BEFORE HIROSHIMA PRISONERS OF WAR IN JAPAN, BURMA AND THE FAR EAST

Dr Jacqueline Jeynes

Stories from Prisoners Of War who worked in mines, on the docks or the Burma Railway, and those that waited for them or lived with them when they came home

First published as "Forgotten Prisoners of War: FEPOWs and their Families" 2015 ISBN: 978-0-9926100-1-2

2nd Edition published as "Before Hiroshima: Forgotten Prisoners of War in Japan, Burma and the Far East" in 2016 ISBN: 978-0-9926100-9-8

In the United Kingdom by

Pen Coed Publishing

14 Water Street, Aberaeron, Ceredigion SA46 0DG, Wales UK

Tel: +44(0)1545 574773

Website: www.pencoedpublishing.co.uk

email: jackiepencoed@gmail.com

Printed by Cambrian Printers, Llanbadarn Fawr, Aberystwyth, Ceredigion, SY23 3TN Wales

Dedication

This book is dedicated to all those who suffered as prisoners of war or interns in the Far East, those that sadly died there and those that returned, and those that waited for them.

In particular, it is dedicated to my Dad who survived his captivity through determination and a never-ending sense of humour. We miss him and are all very proud of him.

Gunner William Albert Halls

1922-1998

Acknowledgements

As with any book, the author is indebted to many people, not least closest family who nod encouragingly in the right places even when you are not making much sense! In other words, thank you to my husband Leslie for his patience and support.

Of course, the starting point for the book is my father, William Albert Halls, who said little about his three years in captivity until a short while before he died in 1998. It is a testament to him that I have finally brought together this base of evidence about life as a Far East Prisoner of War (FEPOW) and of the families who waited for news of their loved ones.

I am, of course, grateful to many individuals and support organisations who have worked with me over the last 25 years to put together their very personal, and often painful, recollections of a period in their lives that is still very fresh in their memories. What began as recording comments from members of the Midlands Association of FEPOW based in and around Birmingham, with the substantial support from Les & Pam Stubbs, extended to meetings with groups of wives and families in Farnham, Portsmouth, Southend and other parts of the UK. Thanks to Doris Lockie all those years ago!

In 1991, I also spoke with Mrs Suzanne Hardiman whose husband was one of Saddam Hussain's hostages in 1990, so thanks to her for her comments regarding the wait for her husband's return.

Support organisations from around the world also spread the word about my research resulting in comments from FEPOWs and families in Canada and Australia as well as the UK. More recently, I have had extensive input from individuals about their memories of when their family member returned from the Far East, the COFEPOW (Children of Far East prisoners of War), Burma Star, Java FEPOW club and other networks have been extremely helpful.

Special thanks go to Jenny Martin who was born in Changi prison; Louise Reynolds nee Cordingly who provided information on the Changi Cross and role of religion in the camps; Ron Wilkinson; Cec Lowry for letters from John Wyatt; Emma Watson with details of her grandfather Harry Leonard Watson; Michael Nellis for copies of documents; Ted Marriott for details of other publications; Maurice Naylor for a copy of a talk given in 2012; William Mundy; Pam Stubbs for her continuing help; Harold Wade; Dr Bill Frankland regarding medical treatment on return; copies of letters from Captain Kenneth Hughes provided by his family; Govan Easton regarding contraband cigarettes!

Information has also been collated during visits to the Imperial War Museum and online contact with The Red Cross (regarding the Changi Quilt). Much of the early material is from newspaper articles and reports – I have tried to list the specific publication details as far as possible although some of it did not carry all the details (especially from the late 1980s) but the Bibliography list includes as much as possible.

I am particularly grateful to Louise for allowing me to reproduce images from her two books, and to all the people I spoke to who kindly gave me copies of personal and official documents.

My sincere thanks go to everyone for their invaluable input.

The Forgotten Prisoners of War – FEPOWs and Their Families

Foreword

Most people think of VE Day in May as the end of World War II, yet it did not officially end until Japan finally surrendered in August 1945 – now known as V-J Day on 15th August. 2015 is the 70th anniversary of the end of WWII and there will be lots of celebrations around VE Day (May). However, I know from experience that there will be less recognition of the Far East Prisoners of War (FEPOWs) who endured a further time in captivity until the treaty was signed between the US and Japan.

The treatment of prisoners of war (POWs) in Japan was particularly cruel and a higher proportion of them died in these camps than those held in Germany. Their personal stories are moving and demonstrate the courage and spirit of every FEPOW. But, the long-term impact spreads much further to include the lives of close family and friends.

This book aims to present the stories of FEPOWs and their loved ones, those that were waiting at home to hear news of what was happening in the Far East during the war, as well as those that lived with them in the years after they were released. Support was negligible, assuming they actually recognised that they needed help and were willing to ask for it. For families, there was no support at all. This book includes reflections from many people over the years, and it is clear that everyone was left to find their own way through these traumatic times.

It is also interesting to note the later discussion about more recent events where civilians or military personnel are held captive, often as hostages for very long periods of time, and how little has changed in the way governments react and families are left to handle the situation.

"We are starving, not melodramatically, but slowly" wrote Eric Cordingly in his diary. "The grim thought comes into one's mind that many of these crosses cover the mortal remains of men reported safe after battle. Men who need not have died but for the facts and conditions of our captivity." (Cordingly L. , 2015)

Contents

1.Introduction

Why this book?

There have been many publications over the years, either personal testaments from POWs, including women and children who were captured, or as an historical record of events in the Far East during WWII. My father was a FEPOW for three years between the ages of 18-21 – as a mother of five sons, I cannot even think about what this means.

However, he survived and was actively involved with support FEPOW groups, despite such organisations being frowned on by the government in the early days after the war. I later became Secretary of the Midland Association of FEPOW groups so gained insight into how each person dealt with their time in captivity and, crucially, how their families coped during the war and after their return.

While individual stories vary according to how and where they were captured, treatment was generally the same – namely cruelty, starvation and a total disregard for human life by their captors. The more I spoke with wives and families of FEPOWs, it became clear that their experiences were also similar, both during and after the war. No support, no recognition of the condition POWs were in on their return or the long-term impact of their experiences on wider family members and, crucially, a cynical lack of acknowledgement of how bad it had been for Japanese POWs in particular.

Why telling their story is important.

Although my father didn't personally talk about his experiences until a year or so before his death in 1998, as Welfare Officer he was crucially aware of how ex-POWs and their families were still trying to cope with the aftermath of their time in prison camps.

At the same time, the Gulf War had finished in 1991 and returning soldiers were showing extreme signs of Post-Traumatic Stress Disorder (PTSD). The article in the Daily Mirror (Todd, 1991) seemed to emphasise the links with previous conflicts, especially the reference to wives who 'lost their men AFTER war is won'.

At this time, I had already been chatting with wives of FEPOWs and realised that little had been said about how families coped with spouses or sons missing and later assumed to be POWs in the Far East, or indeed the civilian women and children in captivity.

This therefore became a more formal collection of anecdotal evidence, gradually building a wider picture of the families during and after the war. I visited many support groups around the UK and also made contact with families in Canada and Australia. In 1997, I was invited to lay the wreath at the Remembrance Day service in Tokyo, representing British prisoners of war who had not returned home and those who still suffered from the effects of the treatment they received.

Unfortunately, this was before the widespread use of the internet and social media, so by today's standards the research is limited to verbal and written communications. However, it still provides a unique insight into the personal experiences of those who lived through WWII in the Far East region – often referred to as the forgotten POWs –and who waited even longer than POWs in Europe to return to their families.

Why now?

In 2015, the 70th anniversary of the end of the war, there will be many remembrance events and celebrations of victory over adversaries. I believe this is an ideal time to present the human aspects of the brutal captivity of soldiers in the Far East, particularly Japan.

Based on the research talking with wives and families of FEPOWs, and some from more recent conflicts, there is a considerable amount of unique data to draw on. Given the age of those who were captured, the support work continues through a combination of groups such as regional FEPOW associations, the Java FEPOW Club, the Burma Star, the FEPOW Fellowship and regional groups of COFEPOWs, the children of prisoners of war. As we continue to engage in conflict, there are also parallels that can be drawn where hostages are held for many years, the potential impact on them and their families similar to those of FEPOWs.

I would like to say that perhaps "lessons have been learned" but, as we know, these are meaningless sentiments that rarely result in appropriate action being taken!

2. The Conflict in the Far East

Brief Timeline

- 1937 – Japan invaded China
- 1938 – controlled Amoy in southern China
- 1941 7-8 December Japan attacks Pearl Harbour
- 1941 Japan attacks Hong Kong which capitulates on Christmas Day. They then enter Burma
- 1942 – Japan invades the Dutch East Indies
- 1942 – February – Singapore surrenders to the Japanese; Japanese land in Java
- 1942 – May – POWs in A Force sail to Burma
- 1942 – July – B Force sails to North Borneo
- 1943 – March – D Force goes by train to Thailand, followed by F and H Forces
- 1943 – March – E Force sails to North Borneo
- 1943 – October – both ends of Thai-Burma railway meet at Konkoita
- 1943 – December – survivors of F Force return to Singapore
- 1944 – American forces return to the Philippines
- 1945 – August 6th – Atomic bomb on Hiroshima
- 1945 – August 9th – Atomic bomb on Nagasaki
- 1945 – September 2nd – Japanese sign official surrender

How it all started

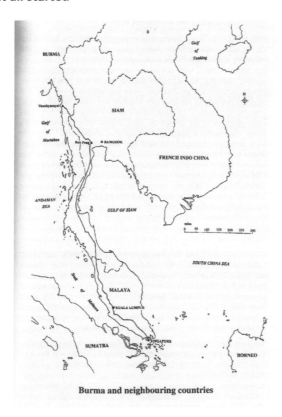

Burma and neighbouring countries

While the war in Europe was well underway from 1939, no-one recognised the extent to which Japan was preparing for its proposed reign over the whole of South-East Asia. After all, they had invaded China in 1937, took control of Amoy in Southern China in May 1938, and by the end of that year they were just 45 kilometres from Hong Kong. By 1941 they occupied the whole of Indo-China (Tett, 2002).

There is a lot of evidence in official documents, diaries and letters from serving men in the region, and commentators in Britain, America and Canada about the way decisions were taken to defend Hong Kong and later Singapore, the majority of this commentary being extremely critical about the whole venture. (Critchley, 1991) (Morris, 1987).

For example, Sir John Hammerton was mentioned in an article (War Illustrated published in WWII) as saying about the possibility of an attack by the Japanese "Presuming that they delivered their onslaught by land, sea and air together, their forces would encounter the determined resistance of a great fortress, a navy of strength at which we can only guess….an army which has recently been reinforced…and an Air Force much more than a match for Japan's". Not quite a true picture of the potential threat.

The article by Jan Morris about the Canadian action in Hong Kong is scathing about decisions made by those in charge – British and Canadian military and political personnel alike – and makes depressing reading into how so many soldiers were killed or taken prisoner unnecessarily (Morris, 1987).

The history behind Hong Kong as a British colony is the crucial factor, as we know, especially the Imperial mind-set of the British government – and Churchill in particular - and the refusal to see that it was not manned, equipped or protected sufficiently if the Japanese decided to attack. Hindsight is great, but even those who were stationed there had made it clear that the supposed defences were grossly inadequate if they were attacked from the north.

The Allied forces had personnel stationed in various places in the region, and in the early days of the war, Canada also considered Hong Kong to be quite safe so used this area to train their young soldiers. Sadly, 550 of them were lost during the fighting when many British and other troops were captured.

There is clearly much resentment, quite rightly I think, about the decision by General Grasett, a Canadian commander, to suggest that an extra couple of battalions of men would make Hong Kong defensible if the Japanese decided to come from the north.

1,975 inexperienced recruits who had never fought in battle were sent from Canada to a tropical, rough terrain they were ill prepared for in October 1941. Within 3 weeks they were in the midst of ferocious battle with little 'coherent strategy' to their defence action. By Christmas 1941 the battle was lost and Hong Kong was surrendered.

Nearly a quarter of the Canadian soldiers were lost even as they surrendered, and the rest taken prisoner. Overall, "4,400 men were killed, wounded or missing, but more than 11,000 survived" and were taken prisoner (Morris, 1987).

An interesting article by Julian Critchley (Critchley, 1991) points out how clues were missed by President Roosevelt and Congress of USA as early as summer of 1940. They had cracked the Japanese diplomatic code so were able to monitor private communications across the globe. Even though their own ambassador in Tokyo had heard rumours of a potential attack on Pearl Harbour, this was still ignored particularly as there had been no official declaration of war by the Japanese.

The attack on Pearl Harbour in December 1941 was, of course, an obvious declaration of war and, crucially, the point at which America had to join in hostilities.

'Dec 21-41 L/C J Wyatt   D Coy British Battalion   Malaya

Dear Mum & Dad & Elsie,

Hope this find you as safe and as well as I am at present. Before I start you will notice that my address is completely changed also that I think it best that you should all just send me occasional letter as all your letters have not reached me now for over a month and as things are they will take a long time to reach me so one now and again to let me know how you all are. Well mum before I start I would like you all to give thanks to God at church for the mercy he has shown not only to me but to the whole Battalion. 3 times I have just waited for death but with Gods help I am still here. I have felt all along that with all your prayers God would keep me safe. I will only give you one instance of it. 10 of us were in a trench in a little native village in the jungle, we were told last man last round for we were surrounded by the Japanese, and they were closing in on all sides, some of the chaps were saying good-bye to each other, and I was really frightened at the thought of dying, but as the minutes dragged on I resigned myself to it then all of a sudden 3 aircraft came over, was they ours? Was they be buggered down came the bombs all round us all we could do as we crouched there was to wait for one to hit us, but that good old trench saved our lives for it rocked and swayed with the impact, about one minute after they flew off, 4 tanks rumbled up the road, and gave our positions hell. They flung everything at us grenades, machine guns, but we still crouched in that little trench we could not return fire for if we showed our heads above the trench the advancing Japs were machine gunning us, all of a sudden, we heard a shout run for it lads, did we run, but the last I saw of the brave officer who said it, I shall never forget him, as we ran past him pistol in hand pointing at the Japs holding them off while we got away. I haven't seen him since. Anyway we waded through about a mile of paddy with bullets whistling past all the time, but we reached the jungle and safety, then on to find the British lines, we tramped 30 miles that day living on jungle fruits. The fight started at 7 in the morning we reached safety at five at night. Then for sleep, food, clean clothes an shave, for we had been at the front for 8

The Independent 16/11/91   letter home December 1941

By the end of 1941, 60,000 Japanese troops took control of the Malay Peninsular and Singapore, capturing 137,000

British and Indian troops. A letter home from J Wyatt in December 1941 describes how he and a group of 9 others fought the Japanese desperately as part of the Battle of Kampar, a few of them only just escaping with their lives "tramping 30 miles that day" to reach the British lines.

Singapore fell soon after Hong Kong, the Causeway between the island and mainland blown up but still the Japanese advanced – much to the surprise of military leaders who thought it highly unlikely that they would be able to advance so quickly and across such difficult terrain. (Wilkinson)

It is clear that preparations for any sort of defence of Singapore were woefully inadequate, and when plans were made to construct a naval base at the north of the island (started in 1929) you wonder why their view of how long reinforcements might take to reach the area was considered acceptable at 140 days!

David Tett's book on postal services in this region during WWII gives a fascinating insight into what was actually happening on the ground, movements of prisoners and military, but it also includes an excellent summary of the build up to hostilities (Tett, 2002). He states that there were nearly 89,000 men in Singapore ready to defend it "to the death" according to orders from several High Command officers, but their biggest problem was lack of equipment, support or fixed defences. Clearly, a ready-made disaster as we know.

The Changi Connection D.Tett

February 1942 saw the invasion of Singapore. Although many people had been warned earlier to evacuate the island, few did so and were then caught up in fighting, slaughter of hospital staff and patients, and ultimately taken prisoner (see later chapters).

By the end of the following year, the Japanese were in possession of most of South East Asia. As Churchill himself noted later, it was indeed "the worst disaster and largest capitulation in British history". How true!

A Japanese version of events

Another version of events, though still reflecting what we have already seen from other sources, is the book by Colonel Masanobu Tsuji (translated by Margaret E Lake) who was directly involved in the conflict. As the cover note says, there is "much in this volume that will be of interest to historians".

"The Capture of Singapore 1942: Japan's greatest victory, Britain's worst defeat" was published in 1997 (Tsuji, 1997)and gives a very clear picture of how the Japanese viewed these events at the time. He notes:

A few themes emerge that are as timeless as war itself: the difficulties of coordinating different branches of the armed forces, endless logistical problems, harsh terrain and unpredictable weather, squabbling between units for precedence and the "fog of war" that renders first reports from the battlefield unreliable".

I think we all relate to those statements whichever side of a conflict you take, and actually are very similar to those stated in translations of The Peloponese War from Ancient Greece in 450BC!

Basically, the Japanese became stronger as they advanced not least because the British did not destroy supplies they left behind in retreat. For example, there were stores of thousands of tons of fuel oil in tanks. Singapore was the British point of domination in the region, and boasted that it was "an impregnable fortress".

The weakness in British plans, as we know, was the route from the north (the Jahore front), thought to be impregnable and unlikely to be taken by the advancing army due to the long distances through dense jungle in intense heat. Churchill believed defences were in place – clearly not the case, and the question still seems to be why was he convinced that they were?

The Japanese plan (according to Tsuji) was the capture of approximately 30,000 though in reality it was twice that in fighting strength and numbers had to be revised very quickly. The overall population was soon more than a million as many fleeing refugees had also arrived there. There was obviously not enough food for all these people for very long so a weakness that was soon identified by the Japanese.

As Tsuji says, there were some sea-front defences but the rear defences were flimsy and hurriedly put together. This left the Causeway a critical point to destroy as it linked with the reservoir. Their plan was to *"crush the enemy to the north of Jahore Strait, to block them in the sector east of the Dyke Road (Causeway), to assault from the Causeway to the west. They would then advance first to the strategic line on the heights of Bukit Timali, and after that to occupy the whole island"*.

Although they had advised Hong Kong of their intentions beforehand, and the opportunity to surrender, this was not the case with Singapore. They used the Imperial Palace as their headquarters. When the British surrendered, they were asked why they had not shelled the Imperial Palace. They said it was because they didn't think such a distinctive building would realistically be used as an army headquarters

- another example of an unrealistic appreciation of the enemy and the overall situation.

When the Japanese entered the British barracks, they found fresh food still on tables – a sign of how unexpected the assault had been. Notes were dropped by air advising the British to surrender, stressing the continued danger to civilians if they did not. After 70 days of fighting, on 15th February 1942, the British commander, Lt-General Percival met with the Japanese to agree terms of surrender and ask for *"a guarantee of the safety of the lives of the English and Australians who remain in the city"*. This was agreed, though as we know these terms were not fully met (Tsuji, 1997).

Capture

As we know, the threat of war had been building up in the Far East since Japan had taken control of large areas of Indo-China. Pat Aspromourgos sent me a letter from Australia many years ago describing how her father, Staff Sergeant Gerald Golledge was stationed in Hong Kong. In 1940, she and her mother were evacuated to Australia via the Philippines, although many others did not see the urgency of the situation in time to leave safely. Her father was captured when Hong Kong capitulated.

Another wife told how her husband was taken in Hong Kong on Christmas day 1941 and was a POW until the end of the war. Later he told her he had led a group of men to the hills but was captured by the Japanese who threatened to behead him. Fortunately, they did not. He was "missing" for 17 months before she was notified by the Royal Marines of his whereabouts – he was in Osaka by now.

She knew that some had escaped from Hong Kong, and she wrote "to anyone and everyone" to try and find out about her husband. Francis also remembered Sir Anthony Eden had announced in Parliament about the atrocities being carried out against FEPOWs at which point she became hysterical and her father told her off!

Harry Watson died in Palembang POW Camp, Sumatra in 1944 as a Japanese Prisoner of War. Prior to capture he was at H.M. Naval Base, Singapore, so it seems possible that he was in the Navy There is a bible belonging to Harry which he wrote in while in captivity. [posted on COFEPOW site in search for family of Harry Watson].

The grand-daughter of Harry Watson was surprised to find that there was a Bible belonging to him so the work of COFEPOW has been extremely helpful over the years, connecting people and gathering data on individuals who were involved in the conflict. Emma sent the following summary based on the details she has, but as with any FEPOWs mentioned in this book, do contact COFEPOW if you can add further to our knowledge.

As I understand, the Admiralty never sent victualling staff overseas but made an exception due to the Singapore naval base being so far away. Harry [Harry Leonard Watson] and a colleague drew straws over who would go to India and who would go to Singapore, so he was posted to Singapore Naval Base as Senior Victualling Store Officer. His son, Jeremy was born in 1940 and plans for his family to follow him out to Singapore were thwarted as the City fell to the Japanese. He was at the naval base when it fell, was captured, and at some stage was sent to Palembang. [grand-daughter Emma Watson].

My father left for Singapore in 1938 and was with the 9th Coast regiment of the Royal Artillery, serving with the 15" Guns of Jahore Coastal Battery. He was a FEPOW from 15th February 1942 until 18th August 1945 and worked on the "Death Railway" like so many others, at various Camps within Thailand [Siam]. [M Nellis]

Ron Wilkinson recalls that when he arrived in Singapore on 11th November 1941, there was no sign of war activity but this all changed on 8th December when the Japanese started to bomb the city. He joined others ordered to go north, crossing to Jahore on 12th December only to be pushed back to the island by the advancing Japanese army. As he says

"Blowing up the Causeway was a futile attempt to stop the advance. They landed on the north-west coast in a swamp area that surprised out leaders". On surrender, Ron was marched to Changi alongside thousands of other POWs (Wilkinson, A Guest of the Japanese Government, 1997).

Ron Wilkinson Peshawar 1941

FEPOW Chaplain Eric Cordingly kept a record of most of his time in captivity, in the early days in Changi typing the notes then later scribbling on anything he could get his hands on, including a child's exercise book. By the later years, any form of written or drawn communication was prohibited by the Japanese so if a POW was caught by a guard, this resulted in terrible punishments (Cordingly E. , 2015).

Eric arrived with the 18th division days before Singapore's final stand. It was to be a short battle. Japanese forces invaded the island and broke into Alexandra Hospital killing doctors, nurses, a chaplain and more than 200 patients in their beds. There is a particularly harrowing description of the events at Alexandra written by Jeff Partridge PhD based on his research (Partridge, 2001).

Newspaper article by Jeff Partridge PhD

He refers to two massacres, one on 14th February carrying over to the next day. The first rush of Japanese soldiers resulted in *"50 dead and many more wounded strewn throughout the hospital"* and was quickly followed by shelling of the building. Men who ran from the building were shot down and those held prisoner cleaned up the wards.

The Japanese refused to acknowledge the Red Cross symbols denoting medical sanctuary, attacking an operating theatre and killing a patient on the operating table as well as several of the medical staff. Worse was to come as 200 surrendered men, including hospital staff and walking wounded, were tied together in groups of eight and were then joined by a group of 60 officers.

After being herded a quarter of a mile up the road, they were packed into three small rooms. *"The doors were barricaded with lengths of wood and the windows shuttered and nailed up. There was no ventilation."* By the morning several had been overcome by dehydration, but a Japanese soldier opened the door and took them out in pairs saying *"We are taking you behind the lines. You will get water on the way."*

More than 100 of the men were led out like this but it soon became clear that they had all been massacred by bayonet. (Partridge, 2001). We know that this was in the early stages of the surrender of Singapore, and that the Japanese viewed the act of surrender as a sign of weakness – these soldiers were of no consequence if they did not fight to the death. However, it still appears as a senseless act of cruelty that bears no resemblance to any notion of "honour".

Fred Freeman's story of his capture and time in Java and Sumatra gives a similar picture. He and a comrade, Derek, were in Java and sent to a sugar refinery at Purwakarta. They were on the first of two trains that were ambushed by the Japanese, but had no weapons to defend themselves. After an air strike, they abandoned the train and started walking alongside the track until they reached a bridge. As they started to cross, it blew up.

He says that about 200 men were lost that night, including the wounded from the ambush left in a hut with some medical staff only to be killed by bayonet by Japanese soldiers. Fred later met up with the only survivor from that massacre who, with 13 bayonet wounds, had pretended to be dead. They were eventually picked up and sent by train to Tasikmalaya, marched into a school building, then told they were now POWs as Java had capitulated. (Freeman)

At the same time, Bob Haynes, Bob Chapman and Ron Thompson were on the second train and were also ambushed with many casualties. They left some badly-injured men in a Chinese farmhouse nearby but later found these men had also been killed by bayonet. Only one man, Johnny Goodfellow, escaped through the window and hid in a nearby barn, although he did give himself up later at Kampang jail.

With Britain's commanding general surrendering to Japan on 15th February 1942, Eric Cordingly felt that this was indeed the time that a chaplain "so useless in combat" would be at his most valuable to the men held captive. We will see later how important the role of religion was during this time. In April 1943, he was sent from Singapore to Thailand as part of "F" Force, only to find the promises of "blankets and even gramophones" to be a distinct lie.

International disgrace: Japanese prisoners of war on the Burmese railway

Work on the Thai-Burma Railway

Instead, F Force worked on the Burma Railway. Within the first 4 months, 90% of the men were sick and by the end 45% had died. He actually spent most of the year in the Kanchanaburi area, close to the railway, and when the main work on the railway was finished towards the end of 1943, he stayed on at the field hospital.

 A similar story is told by Padre John Noel Duckworth. In September 1945, he wrote a moving account of his capture and time as a FEPOW – the full copy was featured in COFEPOW newsletter in 1999 (Duckworth, 1999) – and was broadcast from MS Sobienski in October 1945.

The Japanese told us we were going to a health resort. We were delighted. They told us to take pianos and gramophone records. They would supply the gramophones. We were overjoyed and we took them...They said "send the sick. It will do them good" and we believed them so we took them all.

They were, of course, deceived by the Japanese. After 5 days and nights in metal goods wagons, they arrived in Bampong station in Thailand. They then marched *"or rather dragged themselves for 17 weary nights, 220 miles through the jungles of Thailand."*

There were 1680 POWs who arrived at No 2 Camp Sangria though only 250 survived to the end of hostilities. Fred Freeman told a similar story when they were sent to Haruku in 1943, told they would have *"a perfect camp with electric light, running water and brick billets"*. When they arrived, there was actually the framework for two huts and a pile of bamboo. Rainy season in this region being 300 out of 365 days, life was exceptionally miserable until some sort of shelter was erected (Freeman).

Though due to work on the airfield, after just two weeks dysentery struck and between 20-30 men a day died from the disease. Fred had it eight times in all and weighed just 5 stone by the end. As Fred says *"it's no fun when you hear your bed mate 18inches away die alongside you."*

While approximately 100,000 romushas and 12,000 POWs lost their lives working on the railway, during the construction of the Pakanbaroe railway, 673 Allied POWs and 80,000 romushas lost their lives.

Ships sunk through Allied action

In the first instance, it is estimated that around 87,000 prisoners of war were taken and eventually 4,500 civilians were interned (Tett, 2002). They sent 60,000 British, Dutch and Australian POWs to Thailand from Singapore and Java to help build the Burma railway. Due to the difficult terrain, they were transported in cattle trucks, many of them sick already, in heat and cramped conditions travelling for around 5 days. Others were sent by sea to Rangoon where they worked on the track to meet those working from the opposite direction. (J Chalker)

Prisoners were transported to Japan cross the China Sea by ship, sometimes old un-seaworthy vessels likely to sink, always unmarked as POW carriers. There are many stories from survivors where they were crammed below decks, often in battened down holds so that they could not escape, and targeted by Allied bombers, particularly US bombers (*for example, the Lisbon Maru*). Many ships were sunk with few prisoners able to escape. Those that managed to break out from the holds were met by a handful of Japanese soldiers ready to gun them down. There is a list of vessels sunk at the end of the book.

Some managed to escape captivity during the fighting, often in small groups using whatever craft they could find. Unfortunately, even if they managed to reach shore with safe haven from Chinese locals, Japanese soldiers searched along these shores and small islands to kill or capture them.

In September 1944, Allied forces sank three Japanese steamships carrying supplies, but unknown to them, these ships were carrying (POWs) and Javanese slave labourers (romushas).The sinking of the Kachidoki Maru and the Rakuyo Maru meant that there were now eyewitness accounts from survivors about conditions on the Thailand-Burma railway. Just these two ships resulted in more than 7,000 men dying unnecessarily.

Suffering severe illness, starvation and deprivation, the men were crammed into the holds of the ships with the hatches closed - 'a layer of men lying shoulder to shoulder' (noted by Australian Private Philip Beilby) and a platform above them containing another layer of men. At 5.00am on 12 September, torpedoes from USS *Sealion* hit the *Rakuyo Maru.*

Rivers of fire were blazing in the sea from the convoy's oil tankers that had been hit earlier in the night, but the men knew that they needed to abandon ship. There were very few lifejackets and the Japanese had commandeered the lifeboats. POWs threw anything in the water that would float - pieces of wood, rubber - remembering to collect water bottles before they jumped.

The crude oil made the men vomit as they ingested it and it burned - as the salt water did - when it made contact with fissures and ulcers on their skin. But the oil also created a thick greasy coating that those who spent several days at sea believed gave them some additional protection from the harsh sun during the day and the bitter wind at night. Surviving men would watch from the water, trying to avoid the pull from the ship as the Rakuyo Maru sank the following afternoon.

It was six days before Private Beilby and some others were rescued from the sea by the same Allied submarines that had sunk the convoy. He recalls that these days at sea were spent *'absolutely famished for water, the mouth dries up and your tongue sticks to the roof of your mouth'*, all the while staring out at 'pure and crystalline-looking' salt water. While they tried to keep up morale by singing, the sun's glare became *'unbearable, the oil in the eyes burned, the salt water ulcers caused 'itchy patches' and the skin peeled away. Hallucinations caused some men to swim out to ships that were not there - and drown as a result. Others died of thirst, became aggressive, or simply went 'crazy'.* The men had jumped from the *Rakuyo Maru* feeling free because their captors and the bayonets were no longer around them, *'but you're not free really because the bottom of the sea is calling you'* (IWM SR 23824).

In total, 23 ships transporting POWs are thought to have been sunk by Allied forces during the conflict in the Far East, with the loss of nearly 11,000 POWs and thousands of romushas.

At 10.40pm on 12 September, USS *Pampanito* torpedoed the *Kachidoki Maru*. She sank rapidly, within minutes rather than hours, and the 900 men on board had to jump into the sea in the dark. Having struggled to reach the surface and being pushed away from a lifeboat by Japanese guards, Thomas Pounder eventually managed to climb onto a bamboo raft where he spent the rest of the night. Japanese ships returned the following morning to pick up the surviving men so along with over 500 other POWs, Pounder was transferred to the *Kibitsu Maru, where* they continued their journey to mainland Japan and stayed until the end of the war.

After three days patrolling, Allied submarine crews spotted wreckage and debris with men floating on rafts: *'We couldn't recognize them' reported Lieutenant Commander Davis on the Pampanito. 'They were all hollering and screaming at the top of their voices...They were very hard to handle, they were just covered with a heavy oil, all over their bodies, their hands, and we had a devil of a time trying to get them on board, they were slick, couldn't pick them up. They were quite weak and they couldn't help themselves very much...I remember the first one that came up - he actually kissed the man as he pulled him up on deck, he was so happy to get on there. They were quite in a state of hysteria, they had practically given up when they finally got picked up by us'.*

(Lieutenant Commander Landon Davis's full account of rescue is available on the San Francisco Maritime National Park Association's website, as is remarkable edited film footage of the rescue of 157 POWs from the *Rakuyo Maru* sinking, filmed using the USS *Pampanito's* periscope cameras. The original film footage is preserved within US National Archives). [Section taken from on-line information/ Imperial War Museum]

The Sunday Post, July 10, 1960   11

Glasgow Postie's Amazing Experience On A Doomed Ship

ABANDONED and derelict, the sinking cargo ship Lisbon Maru settled lower into the Pacific waters.

The chill October wind howled over her empty decks as she slowly went down.

But the big Japanese vessel was anything but a deserted ship. Huddled helplessly in her holds was a human cargo of hundreds of prisoners.

[article body text, partially illegible]

Forced Down

This was not the end of the allied attacks on Japanese ships, of course, and the Lisbon Maru suffered a similar fate at the end of September 1942. The Sunday Post in 1960 featured the story of Sergeant John Walker of the Royal Scots Fusiliers, a survivor of the sinking of Lisbon Maru (Walker, 1960). The sub-heading of the article gives a vivid picture of what had happened to the 'doomed' ship.

Abandoned and derelict, the sinking cargo ship Lisbon Maru settled lower into the Pacific waters. The chill October wind howled over her empty decks as she slowly went down.

But the big Japanese vessel was anything but a deserted ship. Huddled helplessly in her holds was a human cargo of hundreds of prisoners.

This is a chilling start to the description of what followed for the 1800 POWs who had been drafted for work in mainland Japan. The men were crammed into two holds, 900 in the forward hold with no bedding just a carpet of soil. As we have seen from other statements, men were suffering from dysentery and beri beri, severely malnourished, and in this ship received rations of rice lowered down to them in a bucket.

An American submarine scored a direct hit on the engine room, lights went out and the ship shuddered to a halt. But the men soon heard the hatch covers being battened down and the rush of water into the aft hold. John recalls that shouts from the other hold gradually ceased as all 900 men in there were drowned, the ship starting to list as it filled with water.

Still imprisoned in the hold, they heard another vessel alongside but this just took off the Japanese and ignored the

POWs below. Eventually, they found a weak spot on the hatch covers and broke through to daylight. Sadly, the rush to the ladder shifted the ship still further and men fell, water rushing in to the hold. They did get out.

But, as John says *"The Japs had left behind a 'suicide squad' – one officer and four armed men"* who fired on the emerging prisoners, killing at least one. Once the Japanese soldiers had been despatched, the POWs realised that the ship would sink any minute and everyone had to go overboard. The article states that *"out of the 1800 men on the Lisbon Maru, only 839 survived"*. (Walker, 1960).

A Japanese Hell Ship.
LISBON MARU.   By A. Jackson.
----

1. Late September - Forty Two,
   Farewell - Hong Kong and Shamshuipo,
   Eighteen hundred strong were we,
   Prisoners on the China Sea,
   Four days out towards Nippon,
   On the first October morn,
   A lurking Allied submarine,
   Loosed her "fish" and got us clean,
   And we were left all battened down,
   Like eighteen hundred rats to drown.

2. Six score prisoners pumped in hell,
   Till each exhausted - Fainting, fell,
   For thirty hours they grimly fought,
   To keep her from the grave she sought,
   Freed from below - One struck her bell,
   Ironic touch' The parting knell,
   Then downed she plunged - LISBON MARU,
   With nine hundred onnms of me and you,
   Nothing marks their graves, and yet,
   We won't Forget - We cant forget.

Not all of them managed to get away, but John and a couple of friends swam to islands 7 miles away. As with many other stories of escape from captivity, John was recaptured and sent on to camps in Japan until 1945. Amongst the POWs on Lisbon Maru was Lance Corporal Andrew Jackson. His poem is a poignant reminder of how these men perished. "A Japanese Hell Ship: Lisbon Maru" by A.Jackson

Fred (Freeman) too remembers four men who tried to escape from their camp. They were recaptured and beaten. Two days later, they were lined up in front of everyone and shot. *"The execution was carried out in the Japanese method; they aim at the throat – not the heart – and believe me, it took several volleys to finish them."*

3. Life in Captivity

Life in camp

All prisoners of war are treated poorly, but it is clear that the Japanese were particularly cruel to their prisoners. Dad recalled that each day, prisoners lined up and waited to see whether any of them were chosen to be beheaded, and who it might be this time. Some days it was no-one.

They were given rancid rice to eat and nothing else, sometimes resorting to eating grasses, although apparently there was some rumour that there had been a camp dog at one time that suddenly disappeared! Sadly, many more prisoners died when in captivity in Japan than in other POW camps in Europe.

The role of the Red Cross has always been significant during war. My father did remember there being one visit to his camp by the Red Cross, mainly because they were each given an orange before the inspectors arrived but had it taken away again when they left. However, if Red Cross parcels did manage to get through to camps, they were looted first by the Japanese then what was left was eventually passed on to the prisoners.

In August 1946, a United War Crimes Trial heard evidence from a Japanese officer in charge of rations at a camp in Sumatra that *"65 Japanese guards ate more meat and vegetable in one day than 1200 POWs had in one month."*

Many families never heard from their loved ones for the whole duration of the war, uncertain whether they were alive or dead. Prisoners were supposed to be allowed to send at least one postcard home, to confirm they were alive. This had no detail about where they were being held, just what many believed to be a dictated statement that said they were well and being well treated. Some cards were pre-printed so POWs just blanked out options that did not apply.

IMPERIAL JAPANESE ARMY

Date 23·5·44

Your mails (and) are received with thanks.
My health is (good, usual, poor).
I am ill in hospital.
I am working for pay (I am paid monthly salary).
I am not working.
My best regards to *MUM, DAD, THELMA,*

AND ALL AT HOME.

Yours ever,

Jim.

The POWs were finally allowed to send a postcard home in May 1944.
Tim significantly included the name of the young woman, Thelma,
he had met at a dance three weeks before he left.

Another example is the mother of Lance Corporal Andrew Jackson who kept his brief letter from Osaka camp;

Dear mother, I am again writing to you from Nippon. I am doing alright so do not worry. Hoping the day is not far off when we will meet again. I am in good health. Give my love to all, your loving son A.

Throughout the book, there is reference to the life FEPOWs lived in the camps around Japan and the Indo-China region, and the names of camps will seem to be familiar.

In the first stages of surrender and taking of prisoners, the Japanese High Command issued lots of rules for POWs – see Communique (Cordingly E. , 2015).

COMMUNIQUE

The Japanese High Command has issued the following instructions:—

(i) The existing administrative and economic systems continue to exist, all personnel retaining their present positions for the time being.

(ii) Public utility services should be restored as quickly as possible, and all employees should continue in their normal duties for the time being.

(iii) Wireless communication and broadcasting is prohibited.

(iv) The air defence regulations are to be strictly enforced, with special reference to the control of lighting during the hours of darkness. The "brown out" and "black out" will therefore continue.

(v) No communication with the outside world is permitted.

(vi) No person may leave Singapore Island without permission of the Japanese High Command.

(vii) All institutions and services relating to the public health and the care of the sick must be carefully supervised and any deficiencies made good as quickly as is practicable. The staff should carry on with their normal duties, tending the sick and wounded and prisoners.

(viii) The Japanese Army will afford protection to the civilian population. Civilians should remain in their normal places of residence, unless they have received special permission from the Japanese Army to move.

(ix) There is to be no spying or espionage against the Japanese.

2. The Civil Government is assisting in the restoration of normal conditions in Singapore. Committees will be set up to deal with (a) questions of administration, (b) public health, (c) economics and finance, (d) prisoners of war, (e) military affairs including the public peace, communications, war material and supplies, (f) naval affairs, (g) air affairs. There will also be a Liaison Committee, one of whose duties will be to arrange for the eventual transfer of administration to the Japanese High Command.

3. It is the duty of every man and woman in Singapore to co-operate in the task of restoring order and cleanliness in the town. We owe this to the wounded, for whom the existing facilities are inadequate; we must not allow the appearance of disease to reduce these facilities. We owe it also to all the women and children in the town, to all those who have been bereaved, or have lost all they possess. I am confident that everyone will help.

4. I thank all those who have rendered such devoted service during the past days. I thank the civil population for the way in which they have remained quiet.

T. S. W. THOMAS.

Feb. 16, 1942.

List of rules and prohibitions for POWs issued by Japanese High
Command on Feb 16th 1942, the day following their surrender.

It would also seem that at first, they allowed POWs outside the camps to collect their dead and bury them, sometimes where they were found if their bodies were too difficult to move.

Eric was amongst those collecting identity tags and personal effects, and throughout his captivity he ensured that he kept the most complete records he could of the burials performed. He even made a note of the *"5 Indians buried by Japanese in village behind house (North side). The Indians had been shot with hands tied behind backs"* which he had found very disturbing.

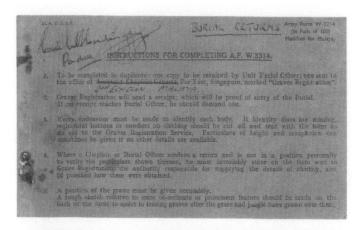

Detailed instructions issued by the British Army in Malaya for the identification and burial of their dead, especially designed for the local conditions. "A rough sketch relative to some co-ordinate should be made to assist in tracing graves after the grass and jungle have grown over them"

Page from Eric's 'Burial Returns' book. For several days after the capitulation, he went out in an ambulance with 6 stretcher bearers to find and bury the dead. On 18th February 1942 he recorded "5 Indians buried by Japanese in village behind houses (N. side). The Indians had been shot with hands tied behind backs"

At first, he also records that they were actually allowed quite a bit of freedom during the first few weeks, even though they were not allowed outside the barbed-wire fencing surrounding their camp. He even records the efforts put into establishing the Church of St George's at Changi which the guards allowed.

As well as regular services, there was a full programme of religious education and preparation for those who wanted to take a more active role in the church and perhaps be ordained. Eric was instrumental in establishing a 'University' for FEPOWs. By the 18th week in captivity, for him he saw it as *"Life is very good, and our position could be so very much worse, we have cause for real gratitude"*.

However, there were also an increasing number of funerals to carry out as sick, injured men struggled without proper medicines (Cordingly E. , 2015). This reference to Changi being one of the better camps was echoed by Ron Wilkinson in his account (Wilkinson, A Guest of the Japanese Government, 1997) below.

Apart from the lack of food, life as a POW in Changi was to prove the best POW existence. Our leaders had negotiated conditions where, apart from daily roll call, we were inside our own compound without direct contact with our captors.

He also refers to there being spare time (clearly a myth in other camps) for social activities, learning and concerts until they were drafted to join others on *"the infamous railway between Bangkok and Moulmein"* 11 months later.

Song That Bridged the Gap: A Yuletide War Memory

ON that Christmas night of 1943, the long, low barrack hut of Amagasaki prison camp, Japan, was crowded. On a platform constructed from two litter-bins and an old table-top, a concert was in progress.

But the acts were not greeted with the usual uproarious response. The choir, after weeks of rehearsal, received only polite applause; the comedians raised only the odd laugh. The audience — although their appetites had been satisfied for the first time in months — appeared indifferent and ill at ease.

True, the festive season had started tragically. On Christmas Eve one of the prisoners had been killed at the factory and throughout the night, members of his unit had kept vigil over the body. That morning the men had congregated in the weak December sunshine while the only officer in the camp conducted the funeral service; and then the body was unceremoniously trundled away in a two-wheeled trailer towed by a bicycle.

Thoughts Were

But that was not the real reason for the men's attitude. Death was not new to them: they viewed it with a complacency bred of hard familiarity. They had seen their friends stricken and die too often for death to affect them for long. It was something far away and not nearby that caused their indifference, their apathy.

This was their third Christmas in captivity. While they revelled in their weekly concerts, this special Christmas edition could not hold their attention. For their thoughts were at home.

They gazed in the direction of the platform, but their eyes did not rest there. They focused on the infinity beyond, storing blankly: each man immersed in his own thoughts.

Effect Was Electric

And then a transformation occurred. On to the platform stepped four men of the 2nd Battalion of The Royal Scots. They sang a song which was vaguely familiar to some and completely unknown to others. But the effect was electric. The men's eyes lost that faraway look; the corners of their mouths uplifted; the smoke-laden air was alive again; the indifference was past.

They still thought of home — of their mothers, fathers, sweethearts, and wives—but their thoughts were put into words by the song. A feeling of peaceful contentment and of security settled over them: they felt in closer contact with their loved ones; and for the remainder of the evening the concert progressed with the usual verve.

Will Never Forget

What was this song that caused the transformation? If you say a carol you will be wrong; although I myself now regard it as a carol whenever I hear it, the sense of Christmas comes about me. But it was not a carol. It was a simple Scottish ballad — "My Ain Folk." It was the first time I had heard it but I will never forget it. Nor will I forget those four boys who sang it and so transformed a Christmas night.

I think of them often, wondering where they may be now. All four as I have said, were of The Royal Scots, but I do not recall them in tartan trews. I remember them as they were that night — muffled up against the December cold in their threadbare suits of khaki serge. But still the aura of tartan hung about them, for they sang the song with the simple nostalgic fervour and sincerity which it demands.

I wonder where they are to-day. Their surnames still I remember; but their Christian names, with the exception of one, are herded under the anonymity of "Jock" — "Jock" Blacky, "Jock" Paton, "Jock" Ramsay, and Mickey Mossaro. They live, or did live, in Edinburgh. I would be grateful if I were able to renew acquaintance with those four boys who transformed a Christmas with a song.

George W. N. Skee

However, George W N Skee recalled a Christmas night in 1943 (Skee) , a copy sent to me by Mr Lockie and a note that he sent a copy to the Royal Scots Museum (above). It describes this Christmas night in Amagasaki prison camp, Japan. In many camps, religious festivals were actually recognised and events allowed by the Japanese, although it is not clear why they did so.

While the prisoners were quieter than normal, George decided this was not because they had just attended the funeral service of a comrade killed at the local factory, his *"body unceremoniously trundled away in a two-wheeled trailer towed by a bicycle"*. As he says, the death of a friend was now commonplace. But everyone seemed to be more distracted than usual as they thought of home.

The transformation came as they listened to a Scottish ballad "My Ain Folk" sung by four members of the Royal Scots. As he says, the words were a true reflection of what every POW was thinking about home. Such things are indeed very powerful when held in captivity.

Given the thousands of FEPOWs, there will inevitably be many instances of good and bad actions by their captors. However, there are several examples of Japanese soldiers actually being kind to prisoners, albeit very few.

For example, Eric mentions that while at the Kanburi hospital camp in Thailand, he mentioned to one of the guards that his portable church organ was still back at Bampong. It then arrived, and Eric describes teaching the guard to play it.

After a day's pathetic wailing of some oriental melody, I have taught him to play Abide with Me, perhaps the first step in conversion from Buddhism. I'm afraid the old hymn tune is being massacred, still it is preferable to his previous efforts.

Eric also gave a talk in 1975 where he gave an example of help he received from a young Japanese soldier who professed to being a Christian rather than Buddhist. Any written materials were banned, so when Eric and an Indian doctor were caught with scraps of scribbled notes from men asking about friends, they were handcuffed together and put down a pit – around 12 foot deep and 4 foot square. In the night the young soldier came down a ladder with a banana each and some sweetened tea for the two captives, telling them to eat them quickly. He then disappeared. It was many hours before the two men were released from the pit.

An example from Clements' book refers to the camp at Semplak, Java where RAF POWs worked to clear the damaged airfield. Selected at random, men had to shift gravel making several trips a day in an old truck. One guard actually stopped the truck in a village and bought each man a cup of coffee and a sweet potato (Clements, 2001).

Despite everyone's efforts to obstruct the orders of the Japanese guards, they did have to be very careful as the notion of 'losing face' was an integral part of the guards' psyche. For instance, if a work party came back with a prisoner missing, this would result in the guard being beaten as he was directly responsible.

They were apparently as cruel to their own troops as they were to prisoners. Recent TV programmes (2015) interviewing surviving FEPOWs and guards gave some touching examples of the cruel training the Japanese had to endure. They were beaten and tortured and the "death is glorious" notion instilled in them.

There was a constant challenge of stealing, hoarding or hiding food and supplies despite the conditions the prisoners survived in each day. In some cases, local villagers were prepared to trade things without the guards knowing, and as we have seen, work on the docks was always going to present some interesting opportunities.

What comes over in all the personal accounts of their captivity, is the resourcefulness of FEPOWs, the inventiveness and sheer doggedness to thwart the enemy at every chance, as well as trying to make the best of what they had. A British Royal Navy POW, George, stated after he was released:

Many of our comrades had died, but undoubtedly there would have been many more but for the adaptability, the cheerfulness and the indefatigable spirit of the British seaman in adversity. (Clements, 2001)

Clearly this applied to all POWs from all the services.

It is also amazing to read about the different ways small goods could be concealed about the person when 'clothing' was so skimpy! One of the most sought-after commodities was paper, whether this was as toilet paper, for writing or sketching records of what happened, or indeed for rolling some form of cigarette. I love the following quote from Eric's diary:

I would not have thought it possible to smoke a block of writing paper [air-mail paper]. I must consider a testimonial to the paper manufacturers ... *"I have smoked your writing paper for the past three weeks and find it in every way satisfactory!"* (Cordingly E. , 2015).

The War Artist Jack Chalker was a FEPOW and made sketches of his surroundings while in various prison camps, as well as the Thai-Burma Railway. These images were produced in dangerous circumstances, secrecy being paramount given the likely punishment if they were found. In the leaflet advertising his exhibition, it confirms reports from other sources, namely:

Conditions were appalling. The staple diet was rice, often with little else, to support working days of 16 hours at a stretch during the 'speedo' period.

During these three years in Thailand to the time of the Japanese capitulation in August 1945, nearly 20,000 British, Australian, Dutch and American POWs died as a result of the railway project together with 90,000 Asian labourers. Thousands more were unaccounted for. (Chalker)

Sometimes he used both sides of scraps of paper, small scale drawings that were hidden inside bamboo buried in the ground, the roof of the hut, in the false section of an army bag and even inside an artificial leg at one stage! Some were lost or damaged by water or insects, but many were saved and formed a major exhibition which was exhibited in London in 1998.

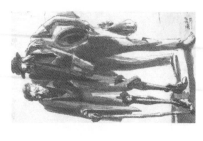

Images
as a
Japanese
Prisoner of War

Jack Chalker ARCA RWA Hon FMAA

The Daiwa Anglo-Japanese Foundation
13/14 Cornwall Terrace, London NW1 4QP
Tel: 0171-486 4348

Private View: Thursday 12th February 1998, 6pm-8pm
Exhibition: 13th February – 24th March 1998
Hours of opening 9am-5pm (Mon-Fri)

to live and work up and down the railway area for three years.

Tropical heat, starvation diet, malaria, dysentry, dengue fever, tropical ulcers, scrub typhus, severe avitaminosis and starvation oedema became immediate enemies, intensified by annual outbreaks of cholera and frequent diptheria. This was in addition to forced labour, injury, and Japanese brutality.

Other parties were sent up by sea from Singapore to Rangoon where they were set to work constructing the track southwards through the Burma border to meet the southern parties working northwards in Thailand.

Conditions were appalling. The staple diet was rice, often with little else, to support working days of sixteen hours at a stretch during the 'speedo' period. Medical supplies in some areas were non-existent in working camps and the mortality rate rose rapidly.

The northern and southern working parties met at the end of ten fearful months and the 414.30km railway was through. From then on it had to be maintained as bands broke down and bridges over transverse gullies on the hillsides collapsed. POW's were engaged on this work until the end of the war. Heavy sick were concentrated in two main Base Hospital Camps at Chungkai and Nakorn Pathom. Thousands of POW's were taken from the railway sites after completion of the work and sent in unmarked cargo vessels to Japan to labour in mines, shipyards and at other industrial activities. Tragically, a very great many of these vessels were sunk in the China Sea en route to Japan, with tremendous loss of life and great hardship, continuing the rapid erosion of numbers of POWs who were still alive.

During these three years in Thailand to the time of the Japanese capitulation in August 1945 nearly 20,000 British, Australian, Dutch and American Prisoners of War died as a result of the railway project together with 90,000 Asian labourers. Thousands more were unaccounted for.

Hiroshima and Nagasaki put an end to this and in addition saved an organised extermination of all POW's had there been an invasion of the Malay

Peninsula by allied troops. It also saved the lives of countless thousands of civilians throughout South East Asia and, perhaps, of well over a million allied troops.

It remains a constant irritant to many Ex-POW's that British Governments post-war, consistently, and perhaps deliberately, avoided any open enquiry or Royal Commission to investigate the gross military and civil complacency and negligence on the part of British Command in Malaya which led to its fall and that of Singapore. It also lead to the greatest and most ignominious defeat in British history and a period of unrelieved horror for the Chinese and Malay civilian population for the following four years. Vital facts have been blandly smothered in a mass of technical detail in official British war histories over the early post-war years.

It is hoped that this Exhibition will show something of the ingenuity and creativity on the part of a wide range of people under difficulties, and, in particular, of the surgeons and doctors to whom so many POW's owe so much. Two great, legendary, and very loved men are particularly honoured and remembered; Lt Col (now Sir Edward) 'Weary' Dunlop, Surgeon, Australian Army Medical Corps, and Capt (Professor) J Markowitz, Surgeon, Canada. It is also hoped that this reminder, 56 years on, of the example of these POW's will help those who view the Exhibition now ever to continue in an endeavour to resolve the causes of conflict wherever it occurs and promote peaceful relations between peoples.

The artist has been helped to organise this Exhibition by AGAPE – the Greek word for unconditional love. It is a charity run by Mrs Keiko Holmes who has been working for nine years to bring healing to Far East Prisoners of War by visiting them all over Britain and taking them to Japan. She also brings Japanese people to Britain to meet POWs in London and holds memorial services of reconciliation annually in the summer.

AGAPE, 35 Leyburn Gardens, Croydon CR0 5NL
Tel: 0181-686 6685 Fax: 0181-680 7472

Jack Chalker was attached to the Australian Army as an official War Artist immediately after the conflict and produced many images as medical records. His collection was donated to the National War Memorial Museum in Canberra. (Chalker)

Movement between camps and jobs was common, men often travelling for many days and nights in cattle trucks or indeed on foot. On the journey to Kinsaiyok, then on to the Three Pagoda Pass near the River Kwai, Ron (Wilkinson, A Guest of the Japanese Government, 1997) recalls a week travelling in a truck to join others who had been working on the rail track. His story also notes his horror when meeting others who had been working there for some time;

This battalion of men, including their officers, were a spent force. To look into their eyes was, to me, one of the saddest experience of my life. There was no spark there. Everyone had a vacant look, as though their spirit had been broken. They were like living corpses. I will never forget, and hope to God I never see this again.

If work was extremely hazardous for the prisoners, just staying in camp was sometimes as hard. The TAG system operated in some camps (including Camp 17) so that every time a POW left his own cubicle/hut, his personal Tag had to be placed on the right nail outside the door to say where he was. If you put it in the wrong place, you had to get it back from the guardhouse.

Punishment for getting it wrong was severe – maybe stood at attention through two or three guard changes, rifle butted, kicked, punched. Ron gives one example when a man was beaten unconscious, sprayed with cold water and thrown into a cell naked. His own lapse in placing the Tag resulted in him standing *"to attention in the freezing cold until roll call the following morning when I had to front up for another day at the factory furnace. Each change of guard produced the bashing mentioned"* It also led to a badly ulcerated mouth for several days afterwards.

I know that my father had all of his teeth smashed by a rifle butt, as did many others. Any other punishments he endured, he never mentioned.

So many illnesses are recorded, many POWs suffering from these debilitating conditions many times before their release (or death). For example, Fred Freeman succumbed to malaria several times:

In this camp I caught malaria, as we had no mosquito nets. This occurred every ten days and the only medicine was powdered quinine bark in its raw state. This was so rough that it tore the linings of our stomachs and touched off the dysentery again. The powder was mixed with 'ongle -ongle' (a paste made from tapioca flour mixed with hot water so that it made it look like wallpaper glue). If you were suffering from malaria, you were given a big ball of the quinine and rolled it into small balls to take at the doctor's recommended rate. When the malaria had run its four day cycle, you reverted to a small dosage as a prophylactic treatment.

A clear description of the condition of POWs, including Fred, was written in 1945 and illustrates how hard their internment had been.

Letter from L/M R.W. Robb – C/NK

…. We arrived back today from a place 100 miles up a river in Sumatra where we went to bring back some of our lads who had been Prisoners of War for three and a half years. Amongst them was a fellow from Brighton. His name was Freeman and …he had been ill-treated and starved all the time. They had had all kinds of illnesses and had had malaria more times than they could remember. Most of them were so

thin you could hardly believe it and next to no clothes and the
majority had had no boots for over three years. They had
been building a railway in some of the worst jungle in the
world with only a small amount of rice to eat and they look as
if they will never be normal again, through the beatings and
slow starvation. Some were even worse than those photos in
Germany and when they were given food they could hardly
eat it. Now they are in hospital in Singapore where they will
get some decent treatment and will go home.

The Selarang Incident

THE SELARANG BARRACKS SQUARE INCIDENT

This incident has been mentioned by many commentators as
a truly dangerous situation for all concerned. The Japanese

High Command issued a form to all POWs at Changi requiring them to sign to swear they would not attempt to escape. Under military law, it was actually illegal to require POWs to sign such a declaration.

They all refused, of course, but this led to "swift and brutal action against the 14,609 troops. (Wilkinson, A Guest of the Japanese Government, 1997). Thousands of POWs, British and Australian, were herded into the square at Selarang Barracks originally used to house a single battalion of men. They held out for 4 days, staying outside in the heat, gradually becoming weaker and weaker.

Finally, with the threat that the sick in hospital would also be brought out to join them, and the very real fear of rapid outbreak of disease, they agreed to sign albeit "under duress". This meant that their signed agreement was not valid anyway and they were still free to attempt escape.

There are various images that show just how desperate conditions were at Selarang, including the makeshift awnings and the Red Cross tents. The printing plate used by the Japanese to print the No Escape document for British and Australian POWs can be seen at the Imperial War Museum (ref souvenirs and ephemera) .

Ron makes a reference in his story (Wilkinson, A Guest of the Japanese Government, 1997) that is not mentioned specifically in other documents I have seen. He says:

I forgot something I feel strongly about, and should not be forgotten, is that the Sikh soldiers deserted and went with the enemy. These deserters were our guards while in Selarang. I personally regard them as the lowest of the low.

Lack of communication

One gunner with the Royal Navy, Dennis Whitehouse, spent the whole of the war in the islands around Port Blair – a POW but not actually imprisoned. As the only European there, with no-where to escape to, they appear to have left him alone. He was found in 1945 when a destroyer landed at Ross Island and arrived back in UK in November that year. He had not been able to communicate with anyone during this time, so there had been no notification to his family. (Tett, 2002)

Tett also notes that there were thousands of Indian and Gurkha soldiers taken prisoner in the region, although there is little remaining evidence of written contact with their families. While more than 20,000 of these POWs were held captive in various camps, it is believed that more than 25,000 joined the newly-established Indian National Army (INA)with the intention of fighting with the Japanese.

This was certainly an uneasy situation for the remaining POWs, and some [Roy Housden in Tett's book] referred to the Sikhs as being particularly vicious as guards once they "changed sides and joined the INA" (Tett, 2002). However, it is also suggested that a British Brigadier encouraged the Indians to join INA to save their own lives.

It is interesting to look at the evidence about lack of communications in the Far East, certainly in the first 18 months after the surrender of Hong Kong and Singapore, where tons of private and business mail kept on arriving but much of it then returned as undeliverable.

Although the Geneva Convention states that every POW should have a postcard to send home to family to confirm his capture and the state of his health, we know this did not happen in the Far East camps. It dictates that this communication should be within a week of arrival at a camp and that it should not be delayed in any way.

The War Office and the British Red Cross were trying their best to locate POWs and to find information about the thousands of "missing" men. Unfortunately, this lack of real information had dire consequences for the families. If he was reported as missing or thought to be dead, payments to his spouse was stopped. If he was thought to be alive as a POW, then payments continued. We can all see how devastating that would be as it was often 2-3 years before news came of those originally thought "missing".

In some cases prisoners were originally reported "missing presumed dead". Mrs Housell told me (1991) of her husband, William Geofffrey Housell BEM who was reported as such, and a memorial service was held for him in the local village hall back home. As she says *"his mother was devastated and died 2 years later. I think the news hastened her death. While he was in captivity, there was no communication or letters on either side"*.

William had been a regular soldier when he first went to India in 1934, aged just 18, but being captured in 1942 he was held POW in Rangoon until his release in 1945. This was a long time to be away from his family and his then fiancée, Cora, so it was even more distressing to find his mother had died while he was away.

A similar story of incorrect information being passed on was from Mr J Boulter. He says *"In 1939 I was newly an orphan with no close relatives alive except an Aunt and cousin. I was in fact reported killed so that stopped any thoughts of me. I never consequently received any post"* (from his letter August 1991). He also noted that his camp only had one delivery of mail during the whole time.

Dear Mrs Jeynes   31 Aug 91

Sorry to be so long in answering your request.

In 1939 I was newly an orphan with no close relatives alive except an Aunt and a Cousin. I was in fact reported killed so that stopped any thoughts of me.

I never consequently received any post. [our camp only had one delivery anyway]

On return to the UK I received a double ration of cheese, bacon etc

It was not until 1944 that HMSO produced a Handbook for the information of Relatives and Friends of PRISONERS OF WAR AND CIVILIANS in Japanese or Japanese Occupied Territory. Mind you, they charged 2pence for it!

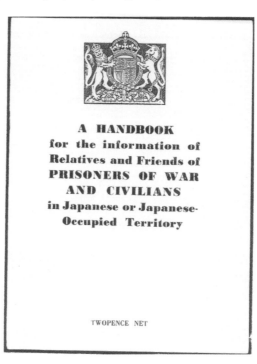

The Post Office did try to help as much as it could, providing standard cards and letters as well as free postage. However, it is clear (Tett, 2002) that much of the post was returned to sender due to incorrect addressing or not including the right things. This was not just returned by Japanese censors, but by British censors before it even left the country.

It would seem to be a bit of a lottery whether you received any mail while in a camp, some receiving letters and cards regularly and others not getting anything. For instance, a sergeant (J Innes) didn't receive his first letters until January 1944, but 22 of them then arrived together. In August that year he got another 44!

In March 1943, there were a reported 5,000 letters delivered to Changi jail – they had received none for over a year before that. Obviously, this contact with home meant so much to the POWs who had no idea what was happening back at home. Delays were inevitable as mail arrived in large bags after being sorted at home, then had to be sorted once they reached Japan, then had to be given to the Japanese censor.

The list produced by David Nelson, in charge of organising distribution of this mail, shows just how far-flung the recipients were likely to be.

The last big mail was completed on the 6th and we set to work bagging and labelling the 'away' parties. Some idea of the field covered may be gained from the schedule below.

Hong Kong	365 letters
Indian camps	50
Java Parties in River Valley Road	90
Philippines	31
Palembang, Sumatra	3,600
Medan, Sumatra	1,596
Padang, Sumatra	500
Java	3,350
Taiwan	1,400
Civilian internees, Singapore	1,235
Local inhabitants, Singapore	1,268
'D' Force, Thailand	8,900
June Mainland, Thailand	6,523
Letter Parties, Oct.-Nov. 1942, Thailand	65,737
Kuching, Sarawak	1,991
Overseas 4.4.42, Saigon	4,570
'G' Force 25.4.43, Japan	197
'J' Force 15.5.43, Japan	559
Keijo, Chosen	196
Shanghai	41
'K' and 'L' Forces, Bam Pong, Thailand	920
Burma—Moulmein camps	61
Dead	19,122
Missing	4,676
Total	126,978

Working prisoners

My father was taken prisoner in Hong Kong aged 18 and was held for three years in various prison camps. During this time, prisoners were moved around and required to work on various projects.

My father worked on the infamous Thai-Burma railway – known as the "Railway of Death" - , in copper mines in Japan, and also in the docks on ship repairs. While he refused to speak about his experiences until the last couple of years before he died, he did always chuckle when talking about the safety of the rivets in the ships' hold!

Clearly, there are many former FEPOWs who are unable to forget what they went through and what they knew to be "unnecessary cruelty" of the guards. One FEPOW who met a Japanese filmmaker in 2001 recalled:

"The conditions were indescribable. We had to march for miles and miles on the railway, sometimes all night. We were working as skeletons. I have seen bodies lying out in the sun and people die from cholera...We had to take people to work on stretchers to die." (Macaulay, 2001)

Hundreds died, and bodies were piled high then burned. The conditions were hard for men who are fit and healthy, so those who had been POWs for longer suffered the most.

Prisoners were also required to help in the locality of their camp. For instance, my father recalled a hurricane and floods in the village around the camp. One night, they were all taken to the local village where an important dignitary lived. Houses were flooded, damaged, villagers were poor and desperately trying to salvage what they could. POWs were instructed to form lines, tie ropes to bamboo supports of the big house and heave them back upright. It was still heavy rain and they were all extremely weak, ill, starved.

But they pulled together and gradually the struts were back upright. As they let go, as if in slow motion, the whole thing collapsed again. A touch of hysteria crept in and they started to laugh, much to the disgust and annoyance of the guards who continued to beat them as they laughed. His sense of the ridiculous is, I believe, what helped him survive!

In no 2 Camp, Sangria they worked every day from 5.00am until 9.00pm, through the monsoons, so that they would receive food rations – remember the sick only received half rations anyway as "No work, no food" was the norm.

"Then came cholera. This turns a full-grown man into an emaciated skeleton overnight. 20, 30, 40 and 50 deaths were the order of the day". Later, he notes *"Presently came dysentery and beri beri – that dreaded disease bred of malnutrition and starvation. Tropical ulcers, diphtheria, mumps and small pox all added to the misery and squalor of the camp on the hillside where water flowed unceasingly through the huts.* (Duckworth, 1999)

He also describes their work existence in very graphic detail. *We were dragged out by the hair to go to work, beaten with bamboo poles and mocked at. We toiled, half naked in the cold, unfriendly rain of Upper Thailand. We had no time to wash and if we did it meant cholera. Our comrades died, we could not honour them even at the graveside because we were still working.*

For 13 months, Ron Wilkinson was based in Camp 17 of the Fukuoka group of camps, Omuta, about 40 miles east of Nagasaki. Here he worked in the very dangerous zinc factory. The tasks *"involved milking the furnace of the moulting zinc which was held in banks of retorts (long ceramic oval cylinders) then recharging these with the raw zinc. The searing heat in front of these banks of retorts was such that after a few minutes at the job, we had to race out and jump into a tank of cold water".*

We can see how hazardous it would be even if they were fit, trained young men but having been on starvation rations for so long, clearly this was an incredible feat that was expected of them. He also points out that

The cotton drill uniform (Jap issue) was no protection against the cold of winter, and always we had cold wet feet in those strange rubber boots with the separated big toe. After the searing heat of the zinc furnaces, the long cold march back to camp was instrumental in many cases of pneumonia, with a consequent death rate of sometimes four men a day.

One POW called Martyn was hit in the face by pieces of a grinding wheel while at work, causing severe extensive damage. Unfortunately, he had to travel by train and on foot to return to camp where he was accused of deliberately injuring himself to get out of work duties. In the end, the medical staff convinced the Commandant that Martyn could not work for a few days, although he was clearly enraged by this result! (Clements, 2001)

The notion of work seems to have been a flexible one depending on which camp prisoners were held in. Patricia Clements' book "Sticky Dewi" (Clements, 2001) is a fascinating collection of snippets from FEPOWs, many illustrating how important humour was to them in desperate circumstances.

Interesting work tasks included requiring the men to each catch 100 blowflies a day which swarmed incessantly around the latrines (page 9). Some would look for the very big specimens and cut them in half, often to exchange for a cigarette!

An Australian, Jack, remembers the tools allocated for their first day's work on the Burma Railway all being gone by the next morning (Clements 2001 page 22). By the time the last plate was to be laid, "gold" rivets had been provided as there was to be great publicity – everyone was given decent clothes and bananas for the public occasion. Unfortunately, these rivets too were stolen, and after the ceremony the clothes and bananas had to be given back. It sounds familiar

– my father recalled the oranges they were all given for a Red Cross visit only to hand them back afterwards.

In some cases, POWs were hired out to industrial companies which contravenes the Geneva Convention – although, as we know the Japanese did not actually ratify their agreement with the convention. They worked on lathes in factories, shipbuilding and loading on the dockyards, but these activities outside the camps provided lots of opportunities for a bit of sabotage – deliberate or unintentional.

"Sticky Dewi" includes lots of examples of such sabotage, particularly where the Japanese were themselves responsible as they appear to have had little knowledge of what the job actually involved (see Chapter 2 in Clements' book!).

Given the poor state of equipment and materials they had available, it is no surprise that so many POWs were killed carrying out these jobs. Apart from work on the railway – where it is estimated a POW died for every rail that was laid – the loading on the docks was extremely hazardous, particularly exposure to coal and cement dust as well as hauling iron-ore in baskets on their shoulders (Clements, 2001).

Actually building or repairing ships gave even more opportunities to make it look like the work was being completed correctly while substituting inferior, or incorrect, rivets. Dad knew that many of the rivets they installed were actually too short and would only hold out for a very short time before becoming loose. By this time, it would be a long way from the docks, they hoped!

Wages for work

There have been lots of different stories about how, or indeed whether, prisoners were paid for the work they did while POWs. There is reference to wages of 25 cents a day at one camp, and some blind or disabled men earning 10 cents a day (the local going wage) for work in a cigarette factory. In other areas, officers had somewhat better treatment and were paid $1 a day whether they worked or not while ordinary soldiers only received their 25 cents if they actually worked (Clements, 2001).

In the early months of his captivity, Eric Cordingly refers to the weekly issue of 9 or 10 cigarettes plus payment *of a daily rate – 25 cents for officers, 15 cents for the NCOs and 10 cents for other ranks.* (Cordingly E. , 2015). At this stage, the men still had personal belongings, such as watches, pens, rings, and they were able to get a little extra money by selling these to locals. This meant they could add a little to their rations, although it didn't last very long.

Fred Freeman, remembering in 1951, said *'Our pay was 15 cents a day and this is a brief idea of the prices on the camps: A needle 2 guilders; a tablespoon of sugar, 20 cents; enough tobacco to roll a cigarette, 20 cents' a spoonful of peanuts, 15 cents; spoon of salt, 30 cents; a page of the bible (to roll cigarette), 20 cents; kitbag (to make shorts) 80 guilders. I have seen a two ounce tin of bully beef go for £3 in English money.* (Freeman)

The role of Religion in the camps

I am grateful to Louise Cordingly for allowing me to reproduce parts of her father's records of his captivity (Cordingly E. , 2015) (Cordingly L. , 2015).

As a Chaplain, Eric was instrumental in offering support to prisoners and, crucially, officiating at so many funerals. There are many quotes throughout this book, but it is also important to explain about the Changi Cross which represented faith and hope for so many FEPOWs.

During his own captivity, Eric consistently sought out places that could be used for prayer. Initially, this was a small, disused Mosque that the men worked hard to make into a place of Christian worship. It became known as St George's Mark I and was a central point of learning and discussion amongst the men, whether they professed themselves 'believers' or not.

As he moved to other camps and hospitals, this format was duplicated to make St George's Mark II in Kanburi near the River Kwai, St George's Mark III in No 2 Working Camp next the Changi jail. This Mark III was moved to the officers' area of the jail near to the chicken runs so became St-George's-in-the-poultry (Mark IV)!

Wherever the church moved to, Eric made sure the Changi Cross went.

What was so special about this cross? Basically, it was an incredible feat of engineering that symbolised the unceasing 'human spirit' in these dark times.

The base was made from a 4.5 howitzer shell case, thick metal that was very difficult to cut, and the four arms from some *"bits of brass from an ordnance gun shop"* (Cordingly L. , 2015). Each arm has a trefoil soldered at the end and a POW Tim Hemmings, just aged 21 at the time, engraved the badges of the four regiments in that 'parish'.

Louise did get to talk to Mr Hemmings during her research and he was fascinated that the cross still existed. It now stands in the Changi Museum and Chapel where they are proud to be the custodians of this remarkable symbol – *a bond to a tragic event almost beyond our understanding* (Jeya Ayadurai, Director, the Changi Museum).

St George's Mark 1, the converted mosque.
Watercolour painting by Lieut Eric Stacy RE 1943

Pencil sketch of St George's Mark II in Kanburi close to the River Kwai.
This "grand little chapel" was built entirely from odds and ends found round the camp.
It had bamboo uprights, grass mats and was roofed with tarpaulin.
Sketched by a POW 1.9 1943

St George's Mark III June '44 – March '45 was constructed in No 2 Working Camp, which was situated immediately to the south and outside Changi Gaol building itself, but within Changi's prison walls. The brass cross can be seen on the altar in both these paintings.
Painting by POW Eric Stacy

St George's Mark IV April – September '45. St George's Mark III was moved to the Officers' Area of Changi Prison. It was surrounded by their chicken runs so it was affectionately known as St-George's-in-the-Poultry.
Painting by POW Eric Stacy

The Changi Cross was designed, constructed and engraved by three prisoners of war in Changi, Singapore in 1942. It was taken home to the UK after the war and brought back to Changi Museum in 1992.

Spreading the Message

There are many examples of art works to illustrate what went on in the camps, and over the years there have been many exhibitions. Many of these drawings and paintings were produced and hidden in jungle camps in Thailand, and recorded events on railway construction. Obviously, materials were difficult to get hold of, and often these images were hidden in sections of bamboo buried in the ground or a host of other imaginative places. Of course, a lot of the work was lost, destroyed by guards or insects, or soaked by monsoon rains. However, as an historical record they are an invaluable reference source.

Fred Seiker's book is made up of his sketches of incidents he witnessed as a FEPOW, many of them showing the torture prisoners had to endure for the slightest misdemeanour, or indeed just for the entertainment of the guards. He was a very gentle man who I met at an exhibition of his work. Punishment included holding a boulder above the head until it was dropped, or the prisoner had to hold it as they kicked his legs or prodded his back with a bayonet. There are also images of the wounds and tropical ulcers prisoners suffered from. (Seiker, 1995)

Another example of the resourcefulness of FEPOWs is The Happiness Box – a book written by an Australian, David Griffin, and illustrated by Leslie Greener. As Christmas approached in 1942, it was clear that the civilian children held at Changi were not likely to receive any gifts so they were surprised to be given permission by the Japanese guards to make some toys. The book is written for small children about three animal friends who want to find the secret to the "Happiness Box".

Unfortunately, the choice of Winston as a name for one of the animals upset the guards so the book was confiscated. Of course, the original copies and illustrations were swiftly hidden! Many years later, it has now been published – contact COFEPOW for more information (editor, 2002) .

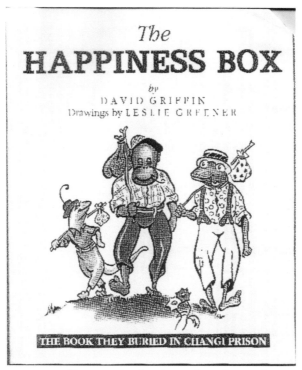

There are many films made that intend to show what actually happened during these war years. I remember when I was very small, my father went to see the premier of "Bridge over the River Kwai" and cried when he saw it.

But, not everyone was happy with the way Lt Col Phillip Toosey was portrayed in the film (played by Alec Guiness) and the difficult decisions he had to make in order to *"ensure that as many of his men as possible should survive their captivity"* (Butterworth, 1991). The recent film "The Railwayman" is based on this story told by a former FEPOW, Eric Lomax, and aims to give a less theatrical version of events.

Perhaps just as significant is the work of the Japanese film-maker, Akinori Suzuki, whose aim in 2001 was to produce a documentary that makes it clear to younger Japanese people exactly what happened during WWII (Macaulay, 2001). He states that there has been little coverage of this in Japan and that many people will be shocked at the atrocities committed.

As we know, there was a lot of criticism about Hirohito (both alive and dead!) in the press, and indeed the Japanese Embassy voiced their disapproval of much of this coverage. But there is evidence of concern from younger generation Japanese who had been given a very narrow picture of what happened during the Japanese campaigns across Indo-China.

For example, Fred Seiker's book Lest we Forget (Seiker, 1995)contains graphic images about how POWs were treated. Fuyoko Nishisato, a young Japanese academic, was determined to bring information about this book to academics and the public in Japan, but permission had been refused for it to be published there. Crucially, Nishisato had wanted to teach students about conditions and the cruel treatment they received, but this was clearly impossible to do (Stubbs, 1997).

Following up long-hidden information, a significant landmark was the publication of the book by Yuki Tanaka featured in the Fulcrum newsletter in 1997 (Titherington, 1997). This tells the story of 656 Australian nurses and British soldiers shot, and 32 other nurses sent to Sumatra to become "comfort women". These were the women taken prisoner all around the region and forced to provide "comfort" to the Japanese soldiers.

It was published in the UK rather than Japan so it is not clear whether it ever reached their shores.

We must also remember that women and children were captured, held separately from the men and also kept in the dark about what was happening to their husbands or fathers. Again, there have been films recorded, such as TV series "Tenko!"(the daily roll call), and some support groups have included meetings for these survivors (see FEPOW Fulcrum newsletters for more details).

Hidden Horrors
Japanese War Crimes in World War II
by
Yuki Tanaka

This book documents, for the first time, some of the hidden atrocities committed by the Japanese in the course of the war in the Far East. The author describes how Japanese soldiers consumed the flesh of their own comrades, as well as that of the Allied military, killed in the fighting. The story is told for the first time of the fate of 656 Australian nurses and British soldiers who were shot by Japanese soldiers. Thirty two other nurses, who landed on another island, were sent to Sumatra to become prostitutes for Japanese military.

The full story is told of the Sandakan Camp in the Borneo jungle in 1945 when thousands of Australian and British prisoners died or were killed. Those who survived were forced to endure a 160 mile march. Anyone who dropped out was shot. Only six escapees lived to tell the tale.

Based on exhaustive research in previously closed archives, this book represents a landmark analysis of Japanese war crimes. There is no denial of the individual and national responsibility for the atrocious conduct of the Japanese troops.

An excellent publication, and well worth the price.

Priced at £20.95 the book is available from:-

Westview Press
12 Hid's Copse Road,
Oxford OX2 9JJ
Tel: 01865-862763

4. Women and Children Interns

Women and children in captivity

There is generally less recognition of the situation for women who were captured in the Far East although there were around 130,000 Western civilians captured, 41,000 of these were women, many of them Dutch ((Archer, 2015).

At the fall of Singapore in 1942, there were many families living there and supporting husbands in diplomatic or military service roles. Clearly, so many women and children as internees was not what the Japanese had planned for and anecdotal evidence notes how they were unsure what to do with them once they were captured. Lavinia Warner commented that there seemed to be no reason for the arbitrary movement of women, viewed as useless mouths, from camp to camp rather than just killing them (Warner, 1982).

The following excerpt is from a talk given by Jenny Martin who was born while her mother was an internee in Changi prison (Martin 2015).

The Japanese army invaded the peninsula and took Singapore on 15th February 1942. Mother was very busy at work up to the last moment burning files in an incinerator at the back of the office. The house had been bombed and they had moved to a flat in Fort Canning. But like many other women she found herself taken, with one suitcase, all she was allowed, containing with other items some muslin nappies, to Changi

Prison. As she was pregnant, she was allowed to ride on a truck with others who were elderly, pregnant or with small children, including her sister Diana who had a little daughter just 8 months old. Their youngest sister Isobel had to walk the long hot trek from Singapore city.

As they approached the gates of the prison, the truck halted and a column of less fortunate women who had walked about 15 miles in the hot sun, marched past into the prison. They were singing, "There'll always be an England, and England shall be free". Mother never forgot that.

This march into Changi was recalled by Robert Brooks in 1999 as he was interned in Changi Jail and later Sime Road Camp as a little boy aged six and a half (Brooks, 1999).

He also noted that the march took place on a *"hot, cloudless day where macadam is so hot that most people walk on grass. But, wearing shoes and being British, the British spirit was maintained. Walk properly, orderly manner, organised and cheerful!"*

While the women sang "There'll always be an England" along the way, he knew that many of them did not see England again and he cannot sing this song even to this day. The march is also remembered in Bernice Archer's book, so clearly it had an impact on everyone who was there! (Archer, 2015)

The majority of women prisoners were taken to Changi, originally a purpose built prison, where women and men were segregated – women in E Block – and boys over the age of 12 were put with the men.

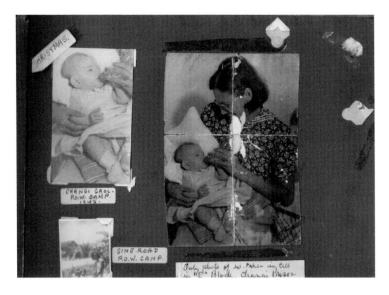

These photographs were sent to me by Jenny Martin. They show her as a tiny baby born in Changi – she did point out that the photograph taken with the baby's bottle was for Japanese PR purposes as it was then taken away again!

The main thing that comes across when reading about their experiences is the way women from diverse backgrounds were now required to live communally, with no privacy. In particular, they survived mainly by living to their individual strengths. Warner (Warner, 1982) notes in her book that the over-riding feeling was that the women generally found much of the experience "rich" and did not hold a long-term hatred of the Japanese as a result.

However, less well-recognised than the prison at Changi, many women were also imprisoned in camps in Sumatra, Borneo, Java and The Philippines and appear to have experienced a much more substantial death rate.

Banka Straits was notorious for Japanese ships sinking those trying to flee to the supposed safety of the Dutch East Indies. Women and children captured were first sent to Muntok, were frequently moved to other camps, then after suffering illness and deprivation found themselves back at Muntok. There appears to be no sign of their existence there now (Warner, 1982).

If survivors managed to swim to shore on Banka Island, they were likely to be massacred on the beach. A woman who survived the line-up of a group at the water's edge was shot through, just above the hips, and eventually got to Muntok. This remarkable woman, Margaret Dryburgh, then gave evidence at War Crimes Trials in Tokyo in 1946.

Changi jail for women internees was not, it seems, quite as desperate as it was for the men.

The British colonial government had been quite proud of Changi, which was quite new, and ironically my mother had been involved in the secretarial work connected with its construction. There was a toilet (Asian squatting type) in each cell, showers, and other facilities. Overcrowding was a problem as cells designed for 1 or 2 prisoners had to hold 4 or more, and a huge shortage of furniture and bedding of every kind and a lot of making do. The kitchens were actually in the men's part of the prison so a huge container of rice was brought through for us twice daily. The sexes were quite strictly segregated and there was much anxiety about what had happened to spouses and other relatives.

Our first commandant [Ishihara] was a relatively humane man and mother got to know him a bit as she was not afraid to go and ask him for things that were needed. She was neither terrified of Japanese people, nor arrogant to them so she could communicate. When the time came for my birth, he arranged for her to go to Kandang Kerbau hospital nearby for her confinement. The European doctors and nurses had all been interned of course, but there were enough Chinese and Indian staff to keep the hospital going. She spent a fortnight there, and was very fortunate that some Chinese friends arranged for an amah to come and look after her, and this lady went down to the kitchens and wheedled the cook for some nourishing food for her (Martin, 2015)

It was overcrowded, of course, and food was poor quality and very limited, but they did have bedding of sorts and some medical supplies. The Red Cross presence seems to have been significant for women POWs at Changi though not so in some of the other prison camps. There was pressure from them to have access to sewing equipment, supplies, and they were even allowed outside the camp to acquire materials.

It also seems that religious festivals were allowed to be recognised, including Christmas and Easter (also see Eric Cordingly's memoires about the Changi Cross). Jenny Martin recalls her mother telling her about the Christmas treat of allowing the women to see their husbands on Christmas day, lining up outside the prison gates and a whistle signalling the men could dash over to see their loved ones!

At Easter, this was repeated and as her father had been sent away from prison at Christmas time, he was back for the Easter treat when he saw his 10 month old daughter for the first time.

While Jenny felt that she was reasonably well looked after, given the meagre rations available to them, this was not necessarily the case in other camps. It was commented on by Sister Catherinia (Warner, 1982) that orphans who arrived at Muntok were generally normal, lively children but they soon became "like old men and women with no strength but to sit down and wonder what they would have to eat that day".

The Changi Quilts

This is an exceptional piece of evidence from Changi and a testament to the fortitude of the women interred for so long. The quilt is held in the Red Cross museum, so thanks go to the Red Cross for allowing us to reproduce the images.

As garments rotted or wore out, they were reworked into clothes for the children. Any remaining scraps were incorporated into embroideries and the women also used rice sacking, hankies, pillow cases, tray cloths – anything they could stitch – in order to record their experiences. They used these unique textiles to "record their internment and at the same time created memorials to those who were interned" (Archer, 2015).

The Changi Quilt is made up of various squares stitched together, each depicting a scene or symbols that hold special meaning to the women producing it plus her signature. For example, there are scenes of a room remembered, hills of Tipperary, flowers and trees, toys and pretty dresses.

There were other quilts and stitched pieces produced by women POWs – extraordinary considering how precious any scraps of fabric were and the ingenious approach to finding threads and, indeed, needles! Each one tells a tale.

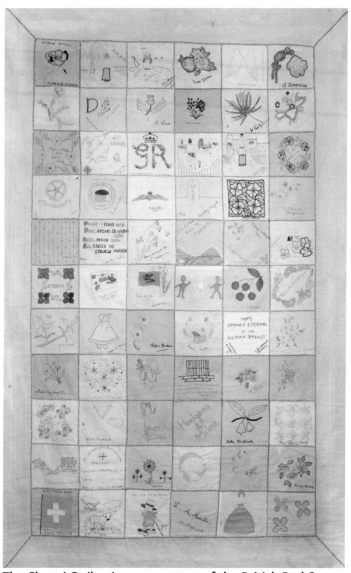

The Changi Quilt – image courtesy of the British Red Cross

Bernice Archer in her study (Archer, 2015) describes many examples, and includes images of these that are either on show in museums, or held by the families of the women. The Imperial War Museum in London also has images of embroidered work you can see. For example, there is a tray cloth that shows Changi prison, includes significant dates and a note "9 miles" (ref IWM EPH 10393).

Hilda Lacey in Changi produced several images on a sheet including the Japanese flag flying over the prison with the words "Flag of Tyranny". She also included a view of one of the cells at the prison and the special event "The dustbin parade"! When men and women prisoners took out the bins, this was the closest they could get to each other so, they often tried to arrange for husbands and wives to actually get a glimpse of each other. It clearly caused some amusement to the prisoners as they wondered what the Japanese thought of men and women all of a sudden wearing their best clothes to take out the rubbish!

Mrs Ada Willies managed to stitch 68 signatures of female inmates at Changi, and by the time the women were moved to Sime Road camp in 1944, 14 year old Vilma, daughter of Theresa Stubbs, used red, white and blue stitching to record signatures of the internees.

Mrs Maudie Hilton was 56 years old when she was captured, and produced some exceptionally fine, tiny embroidered pieces. These included a scene of Singapore on fire, and an image of Banka Strait with Muntok camp and the lighthouse.

There are also scenes of Moesi River and Palembang bungalow camp so these are incredible records of these places. Sadly, she died while a prisoner and her embroidered work was brought back by another internee and given to Mrs Hilton's son.

Generally, the pieces had to be worked on in secret and carefully preserved, hidden from the Japanese soldiers' eyes. Often, they were then part of the women's personal effects when released but families were not always aware of them or their historical significance. If you have any hidden away, please let someone know!

However, the Japanese Commandant actually gave permission for the various Changi Quilts produced during the first 6 months of internment to be given to the Military Hospital at Changi Barracks. This therefore gave some positive news to patients about the women who were still alive in the jail.

It is believed there were actually four quilts produced, one hangs at the British Red Cross museum, and two further quilts hang at the Australian War Memorial Museum in Canberra. It is not clear whether a fourth was actually produced or its current whereabouts. (Cooper C. -e., 1999)

While there were occasionally examples of some kindness from the soldiers, this was rare. The commander at Changi when Jenny was born told her mother that he also had a baby daughter at home that he had not yet seen, so he does appear to have treated them humanely.

Although groups of survivors from boats sunk in Banka Straits were then massacred on the beach, another group who reached the shore were given some coffee by one soldier and an officer provided a nurse dressed only in her corsets with a jacket. Nevertheless, treatment of the women was extremely brutal in some cases.

By the time the war was nearing an end (although clearly prisoners did not know this at the time), rumours had started to circulate that the women moved to Sime Road camp were to be buried in huge pits being dug by the men. It had become impossible for them to be fed, even given the meagre rations they lived on.

These recollections from women who had been civilian internees are an exceptional record, and give valuable insights into how they coped during their time in the Far East. Their voice is often forgotten.

5. The end of the war

Most people think of VE Day in May as the end of World War II, yet it did not officially end until Japan finally surrendered on 14th - 15th August 1945 – now known as V-J Day. The US dropped the atomic bomb on Hiroshima, killing more than 70,000 people, then three days later dropped another bomb on Nagasaki killing a further 40,000. Until this point, the intention had been to "exterminate" all FEPOWs still alive if allied troops on the ground had moved forward on the Malay Peninsular. However, given the scale of the US attacks, Japan surrendered unconditionally to the Allies on board the USS Missouri in Tokyo Bay.

Just before the war ended, every prison camp was issued with the following instructions (now held at the Imperial War Museum) to be carried out if Japan was attacked by Allied forces:

Whether they are destroyed individually or in groups, or however it is done, with mass bombing, poisonous smoke, poisons, drowning, decapitation or what, dispose of them as the situation dictates. In any case, it is the aim not to allow the escape of a single one, to annihilate them all, and not leave any trace.

This, of course, referred to all prisoners of war and internees. This did not happen, as we know, and the reprisals many expected in the camps once the Japanese surrender was confirmed did not take place. There were a few instances of

Japanese soldiers refusing to believe that defeat had happened, and some stories of soldiers who retreated to remote jungle to carry on fighting.

In addition, the Japanese Chief of the Prisoner of War Camps sent a signal to all camps that *"Documents that would be unbearable in the hands of the enemy are to be treated in the same way as secret documents and destroyed"* (Tett, 2002). Most camps destroyed all documents, whether sensitive or not so much of the evidence is down to anecdotal evidence and copies of letters etc kept by the families of FEPOWs.

Liberation

Plans were put in place to rescue the thousands of POWs in camps around the Far East, including many British, American, Canadian and Australian prisoners. My father described the day when they realised the war must be over.

"We suddenly realised the guards were shouting, well screaming really, at each other with lots of running around. Definitely panic in their voices, so we wondered if there were some Allied troops nearby. Then suddenly, it all went quiet and we looked at each other in our hut, waiting for something terrible to happen. But, we could hear the gate creaking, and when I looked out of the window, the whole camp was deserted. Not a Jap soldier anywhere. And the gates were open! Next we heard the drone of planes overhead, and things started to drop from the sky."

When they finally came to rescue my father, there were 50 men left from an original total of 500 in this camp. But again, he chuckled when he said they dropped food parcels before the troops came in to liberate the camp, expecting there to be more men. Even though they had not eaten proper food for so long, they did their best to eat as much as they could manage knowing they would just be sick.

Ron Wilkinson in his story "A guest of the Japanese Government" (Wilkinson) recalls a similar story of the end of hostilities. He remembers they felt the earth tremor from the atom bomb dropped on Nagasaki on 9th August, but everyone thought it was just another earthquake (common in that region). *On 15th August most of the guards left the camp and a holiday was declared. We were told that it was to celebrate their dead enemies. Of course, it was the end but we did not know this until two weeks later when the B29 bombers came over unopposed, flying quite low.*

They dropped *supplies of food and clothing on huge parachutes, and a message to inform us of the end of the war and to stay where we were, and that we would eventually be picked up and taken home.* Sadly, two American POWs were killed during this drop as parachutes failed to open.

Ron was taken by train to Nagasaki on September 15th, shocked by the devastation caused by the bomb as he looked through the windows. But he notes that *"once off the train, medical care was immediate. I was sponged down with a white substance, which killed and removed the hundreds of body lice.* After a "beautiful hot shower" they went on board the hospital ship to a bed with clean white sheets. *"From Hell to Heaven"* he says.

In 2012, Maurice Naylor gave a talk about his experiences of liberation and repatriation. He kindly agreed for me to reproduce part of the talk, so the following extracts give a clear picture of his memories of that time (Naylor, 2012).

In August 1945, I was in a POW camp about 6 miles north of Ubon in Thailand. The camp had been going for some time and held about 2000 prisoners who were required to dig defence works and construct an airstrip. I was quite relieved to be in a well-run camp away from the threat of constant bombing by our allied Air Forces (which had been the case in Bangkok and along the railway since 1944).

The work was not unduly arduous, and we were paid, but there was no sense of urgency. The worry as a prisoner was how on earth would we get out of this situation alive? The second worry was how long would the war last as it had taken six years to defeat the Germans?

In July, work on the airstrip stopped abruptly and we started to dig trenches 10 foot by 6 foot across the airstrip. At the time we did not know it, but the Japanese High Command had ordered the elimination of prisoners of war in the event of an invasion of Malaya or Thailand. We had dug our own graves!

On August 13th three of the Korean guards deserted and there was great confusion amongst the Japs. There were rumours of a new and powerful weapon which had been used on Japan and had caused "black rain" to fall and immense casualties. We did not believe it. Work parties stopped on 15th and 16th August.

The camp seethed with excitement and we were told that the British camp administration believed the war was over. But we were warned to remain calm. At the back of our minds were the trenches dug across the airstrip. To our dismay, work started again on 17th and 18th, but there was obvious confusion in the camp, records and papers were being destroyed. On that evening Major Cheda announced to a full parade of prisoners that the War was over and that we were free men. No fire or brimstone, no gunfire, no bloodshed – just the simple announcement that the war was over. As one FEPOW wrote in his diary "Peace has come to us peacefully – like a dove on quiet wings".

This is a very interesting reflection on how the Japanese soldiers dealt with defeat – there seemed to be no significant reprisals against POWs in most of the camps, rather a shamefaced acceptance that they were defeated. Clearly this was an unexpected result for everyone.

Many of the prisoners were sent on to Canada to recuperate before coming back to Britain, generally because their health was so poor. A naturally tall, well-built man, my father only weighed 5 stone when he came back. His medical records for his War Pension notes he had had dysentery, malaria, malnutrition and beri-beri, pulmonary tuberculosis (the reason we were unable to emigrate to Canada 1952), dental caries and subsequent extractions (teeth broken with Japanese rifle butt), hearing loss and basal cell carcinoma left temple. Clearly, many of these conditions were found in the majority of other FEPOWs on their return.

Awarded for excellence

WAR PENSIONS AGENCY

An executive agency of the Department of Social Security

Your reference is HY106024A
Please tell us this number
if you get in touch with us

Mr William A Halls
64 Linton Park
Linton Lane Bromyard
Hereford
HR7 4LF

WAR PENSIONS AGENCY
NORCROSS
BLACKPOOL
LANCS
FY5 3WP

Our phone number is
01253 858858

Date 16 Apr 1996

About your War Pension

We have decided to keep the assessment of your disablement at 50% from 01/05/96 to 30/04/00 for the following conditions

* BASAL CELL CARCINOMA LEFT TEMPORAL REGION
* DENTAL CARIES WITH SUBSEQUENT EXTRACTIONS
* DYSENTERY
* MALARIA
* MALNUTRITION AND PRIVATION (INCLUDING BERI BERI)
  WITH ASSOCIATED NERVOUS FEATURES
* PULMONARY TUBERCULOSIS

If you think your disablement has got worse

You can ask us to look at your War Pension again. We call this a deterioration claim.

Jenny also recalls the chaos as the hostilities seemed to be coming to an end.

Early in 1945 we were suddenly moved to Sime Road camp, an old RAF camp. Suddenly, everything changed. Unknown to us, a bomb fell on Hiroshima and then another on Nagasaki. One day, the guards all disappeared and then a plane flew overhead and dropped from its undercarriage, thousands of leaflets, fluttering to the ground like snow. Around me everyone was saying "Thank God, thank God!" The leaflet said, "The War is over. Japan has surrendered. We are coming for you very soon. Do not overeat!"

We were taken in trucks to Raffles hotel – not at this time a luxury hotel, but with several camp beds in each room, where forms were filled in and we waited for news of my father and my mother's family in Ipoh. Both my aunts were still with us and my cousin, Genevieve, just a year older than me.

In due course, skeletal men began to arrive from the north, my father among them. He had been sent up work on the railway in Burma, and had suffered like most others, typhoid, beri beri and starvation. But he had survived. (Martin, 2015)

Staff Sergeant Gollidge was held POW in Stanley camp then sent to Osaka in Japan. Although letters were sent regularly to him from his family, his daughter says they had no way to know if he received any of them. As he was so ill with beri beri when the hostilities ended, it was decided to send him home by plane. Pat says *"There was a typhoon at sea and the plane he was in crashed and never recovered. We were all devastated. The war was over and we thought we would all be together again, and then to receive that news was very hard indeed."*

Although the parachute drops had started in August, it was still several months before all POWs were finally transported from the camps. Admiral Lord Mountbatten had been charged with overseeing the repatriation of around 123,000 people from the region – a massive undertaking. Plans were already in place for the Allied troops to take charge of POW camps if further hostilities carried on. The bombing of Hiroshima and Nagasaki brought it all to an abrupt end without these plans being put into practice.

When the Japanese surrendered, Lord Mountbatten was actually handed the sword of Field Marshall Count Terauchi, an event not widely known in later years but mentioned in a small newspaper cutting at the time. It was indeed noteworthy as "it was possibly the last occasion in war when one Supreme Commander surrendered his sword to another" (Cooper, 1999). The blade of this ancient sword was forged in 1292 and was kept at the Admiralty office in London – see Lord Mountbatten's letter.

The leaflet drops were part of this action – 18 million in all over 58 towns and 55 camps across the region in 4 days. By early September, where the Japanese were still at camps, Gurkhas took over to ensure the security of POWs. As well as the Red Cross and RAPWI officials, the press soon arrived so stories started to emerge about the plight of FEPOWs.

Maurice Naylor noted that

"on 30th August two offices and two NCOs from RAPWI (Repatriation of Allied POWs and Internees) were parachuted into camp. But then we had to wait. The potential threat of reprisals by the Japanese failed to materialise and at last, on the 25th September we moved by train to Bangkok and the next day flew to Rangoon" (Naylor, 2012).

However, he also recalls the 6 week journey home on the SS Orbita, arriving in Liverpool on 9th November to a "muted welcome" as they were one of the last ships to arrive. Even this arrival home was frustrating as they were not allowed to disembark and his parents, who had been notified of his expected arrival, were not allowed on board. A very sad welcome, as his parents went home to Manchester without actually seeing him.

WELCOME TO RANGOON ! !

At last the day has come. Three years of darkness and agony have passed, and a new dawn is here, bringing with it for all of us deliverance from danger and anxiety, and for you above all freedom after bondage, the joy of reunion after long separation.

Through these long years we have not forgotten you. You have not been at any time far from the thoughts of those even who had no personal friends or relatives among you. We of the Red Cross have tried every way of establishing contact and relieving your hardships. Some provisions have been sent, and many messages depatched ; but we do not know how much has reached you, for the callous indifference of the enemy has made the task well nigh impossible.

But now that that enemy is beaten and you are free once more, we are doing all we can to give you the welcome you richly deserve and to make your homeward path a pleasant and a joyful one. If our preparations in RANGOON leave something to be desired, it is only because the end has come sooner than we dared to hope and has found us unprepared. These deficiencies will be more than made up by your welcome in India and your homeland.

On behalf of the Indian Red Cross and St. John War Organization we welcome you. May God bless you and send you home rejoicing !

G.B.C.P.O.—No. 34, Army (Asst. R.C.C.), 29-8-45.—12,000—I.

A similar story is told by Kenneth Mitchell Hughes in his letters home to his parents (although sadly he died in hospital in Rangoon) – all POWs were to be flown out of Thailand to Rangoon and then on to India to be transported by ship back to England. As we know, some did not go straight to Britain but went via America or Canada. Of course this was a massive undertaking with so many POWs and Internees, many of them very sick.

C/o. P.O.W. Mail Centre,
Bombay Command.
12th September 1945.

My Dear Mother & Father,

Since the end of the Japanese war I have already written you three letters which have more or less repeated each other. I am now taking it forgranted that you have had at least one of these, so in this letter I shall only give you details of the more recent events.

This is the first letter I have written on British Territory since the fall of Singapore as I am now in Rangoon. I arrived here yesterday by air from Bangkok and am at present in hospital in the centre of Rangoon. Coming to hospital is only a formality where all ex P.O.W's are subject to medical examination. I have never been fitter than I am at present, and you will be glad to know that I was found to be perfectly O.K. by the Medical Officer.

I am expecting to be discharged from hospital in a day or two and will then go to a transit camp awaiting embarkation. We are told several ships are on the way to Rangoon and can expect to have sailed by the end of September at the latest. The ships go straight from Rangoon to England so I am hoping to be with you, with luck, by the end of October or by the latest in early November. It sounds so good that I can scarcely believe it.

The flight from Bangkok to Rangoon was a great experience and only took 2½ hours. Since our arrival here everyone has been very kind to us and the Red Cross people have loaded us up with good things. The first thing we did on arrival was to send a priority cable home stating that we are safe and in British hands, so I hope you have received this message and that it got through to you without delay.

Last night I slept in a proper bed with sheets for the first time for 3½ years - a really wonderful experience. A lot of mail has arrived from home which has come by air mail and many of these have been distributed, so you can guess how excited I am in anticipation of getting one from you and thus making contact with you again as I have'nt heard from you since June 1944.

This must be all for the moment. I shall continue to take every opportunity of writing to keep you in touch with latest developments.

Much love
from
Kenneth.

In contrast, Ron Wilkinson recalled his journey home from Manila across the Pacific to San Francisco. *"Sailing under the Golden Gate Bridge, I witnessed a happy sight. The bridge was lined with people calling out a welcome. Another week of care before boarding the train, in First Class luxury, over the*

*Rockies with many stops where the Americans made us feel
so welcome. The kindness was, to say the least, touching. In
New York we boarded the Queen Mary which took us at great
speed to Southampton."*

In fact, Ron had received a letter from his brother while in
San Francisco telling him his parents had died not long after
they got news that he was missing. Despite this sad news,
Ron was happy to get back to Britain and family but was then
sent to Australia to be with his sister who was officially his
next of kin. Ron believed he was obliged to go as he was still
a serving soldier and *"they are obliged to send you to your
next-of-kin"*. Although initially reluctant to leave, he did
settle in Canberra and started his own family, so a happy
ending for Ron. (Wilkinson, A Guest of the Japanese
Government, 1997)

Repatriation

In all, it took three and a half months for POWs to be
repatriated – very impressive given the size of the task.
However, the Dutch POWs had to wait longer before they
finally got home. They were moved to camps in Singapore
while they were waiting, although they did have food and
were allowed to move around the island as they wished.
Finally, they were all repatriated by March 1946.

In Britain, the Department of the Red Cross and St. John War Organisation produced *The Prisoner of War,* a journal for relatives of men held captive by enemy troops during the Second World War. From February 1944 they added a supplement, a special eight-page edition called *Far East,* so as to distribute information more efficiently to families. Scotland Red Cross produced its own version of the newsletter and in Australia, there was a similar publication produced by the Red Cross.

In March 1945, one of the survivors of the *Rakuyo Maru* wrote a double-page spread to give families *'an idea of what our daily lives were like'*, and he wrote of the work, the punishments and the lack of food.

He explained that there was no chance for anybody to escape, and that once you were caught trying, *'you didn't get another chance'* (IWM E.10426). These survivors were completely unaware that fellow prisoners were still experiencing forced labour along railways and in coal mines.

Although still a very young child, Jenny Martin remembers leaving for home.

We were on the first ship to leave for the UK, the Monowai, which arrived at Liverpool in due course, after a stop at Aden where we were taken thanks to the Red Cross to a huge warehouse full of garments for men, women and children to equip us to return to the October UK.

From Liverpool a train took us to Edinburgh's Caledonian station where my father's sister, Rena, met us and took us to Corstorphine where she lived with my grandmother and we spent Christmas 1945 there with them. There was a tree! Christmas goodies! Even presents! Aged 3 1/2, my first traditional Christmas.

TAKEN ON THE "MONO FIRST SHIP SINGAPOR & P.O.

When Fred Freeman was finally released, his parents were sent the following letter, the standard format sent to the family of survivors.

Air Ministry (Casualty Branch), 73-77

Sir, I am directed to state that information has been received that 916461 LAC F. G. Freeman is safe in allied hands. Although it may be some time before he arrives in the United Kingdom you will doubtless hear from him direct before long. In any case, information of a general character regarding recovered prisoners, including their movements before they reach home, will be given from time to time in the wireless and will be published in the press.

Within a short time after his repatriation, Fred recalled

My weight on going overseas was 10 stone 7 lb. On release my weight was 5 stone 6 lb but since my return I have managed to get up to 9 stone 4 lb. I have had about fifty attacks of malaria and still get them, as well as frequent trouble with my eyes.

They were generally in such poor health, even after a length of recuperation, that people did not recognise them on their return. My grandmother didn't recognise my father when he got off the train in Birmingham, and she ran up and down the platform looking for him.

There seems to have been little real support for individuals once they returned home. Extra clothing and food ration coupons were supplied, although this also seemed to present problems for people when they tried to use them. Mr Boulter does recall getting a double ration of cheese and bacon when he returned to the UK, and many ex-FEPOWs and civilian interns referred to these little extras.

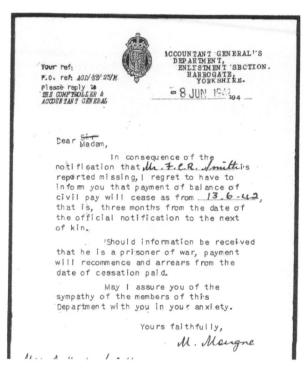

Despite this, there were still some who lived in virtual poverty for many months, either waiting for their husband to return home or while fighting the authorities about money they were owed. The War Office issued a "Restricted" document to all ex-POWs explaining how their pay and terms of service would now continue.

It mentions ration and travel coupons they were entitled to. One area that did cause problems was the assumption that POWs were paid for their labour during captivity, and this 'assumed' amount was then docked from whatever was due to them until proved otherwise. (Office, September 1945)

Memories of homecomings

In the early stages of my research, in late 1980s early 1990s, I spoke to several groups of wives of FEPOWs. They were all very helpful and very positive, although clearly they had all experienced many difficulties as their men returned home.

Mrs Doris Lockie said her husband had been a Regular soldier but time in captivity was not counted for 'length of service'. She was just told that if he was not found within a certain time, her pay would be a Widow's Pension. Once she knew his location as a POW, she could send one letter a month and he did actually receive two of them. When they came home, they were supposed to see a psychiatrist, but even though he was in hospital for five days, no-one saw him. He did see a psychiatrist in mid 1980s, so basically no counselling or support was available to the majority of ex-FEPOWs.

The following comments are from the group rather than an individual, as they felt it helped them to keep it generalised rather than too personal!

- A much smaller percentage of the men were actually married before serving in the Far East (possibly only around 3-5%) and these would have been the older regulars, the majority of the others serving would have been too young
- There were a lot of Chinese girls married to the young British servicemen, though not all with marriage certificates. They had heard that some of these Chinese girls were very badly treated by the Japanese and some were deported to China and the Regions (see also references to Comfort Women)
- The government changed the paybook during the war for some of the women – it now said "W" as a reference. Did this mean "Wife" or "Widow"? No-one told them what it meant
- Family and work were the main means to help them cope as individuals, jobs including working on aircraft in Cambridgeshire, on railways and signals
- It was different for the women depending on whether they were a wife or mother of the POW, especially when they came home – lots of examples of having to deal with nightmares and outbursts of rage (sometimes these were actually violent towards the woman)
- One of the ladies explained that her baby was born in April 1941 so was just 6 months old when her father went overseas – when a toddler she would say "Tokyo's got my daddy". But then when he returned,

it was difficult being accepted by his child as she was used to being the only one in the household
- Her husband was away for 4 years, at least 18 months with no idea where he was, first listed as "missing" in press then "missing believed POW". Whole regiments had been taken so no-one knew who had survived for a long time. This lack of information was definitely the worst to cope with. At one stage, she wrote to the Pope asking him to do something for these prisoners
- When they returned, FEPOWs were told they would be housed first in the new 'prefabs' but they didn't – only a few were given places
- Even with the complete support from the family, for some of the men there was an attitude of "I need to be on my own" – one said that her husband was able to talk about his experiences with someone and that really helped
- People at home did not seem to understand what these men had been through. Quote from an employer at the time "while you have been lazing about in a POW camp, we've been keeping the country going".

Cora Housell explained that it took her husband a long time to get back to normal as he had been so ill-treated, was very thin, and sometimes would cry out in the middle of the night – a familiar story for many wives.

Francis Cole's son was born in 1938, so he was nearly 8 years old before he saw his father again. The needs of both her and her husband were not recognised, not even by family as they didn't realise how they were trying to cope. Her husband expected to go back into normal life but his "nerves were really bad" and it was suggested he got a job in the outdoors.

A gardening job at Burlingham Manor was actually his salvation, as he got stronger, he started to go to church and eventually to meet people in the local pub. She did feel like "piggy in the middle" between her son and husband as they were initially a little jealous of each other, but eventually they became much closer.

As we know, there are typical themes emerging and everyone has a particular memory that stays with them through the years. The comments below are very recent ones from surviving FEPOWs and their families, and it is interesting to see how indifferent people seemed to be back in the UK. Presumably, this was due to a lack of information about what was happening in the Far East and the government's reluctance to pass on any information they did have.

Michael Nellis: *I was 8 years of age when he [my father] returned to the UK and I have very vivid memories of his time, trying to re-adjust to a "Near normal Life"*

William Mundy: *I had very little hassle when I arrived back in England. I was in a Reserved occupation so did not need resettlement. The only incident which comes to mind* concerns the disability pension. The consultant who saw me on my arrival home, a Mr Davenport of St Dunstan's, told me eat as much Marmite as I could, which I did. He saw me again at Uxbridge, before I was demobbed, and told me there was some improvement but it would not now get any better. A little later I saw an Optician at Chatham, under instructions from Ministry of Pensions, who having looked at my eyes commented that they would improve. The next time I saw him he expressed his view on improvement. This meant the pension was reduced. I knew there was no improvement and appealed. This was up held, and pension restored.

FEPOW widow Pam Stubbs, long term supporter of the Birmingham Association of FEPOW and currently Newsletter editor, has written 3 books on the 'Unsung Heroes' from every branch of the armed forces, including detailed data about where they were held captive. She has interviewed almost every widow over the years. She says that *"FEPOWs were all told not to talk about that time and that is possibly why they met locally to have that comradeship though not necessarily to talk about their experiences"*.

Many ladies who were engaged or married to the men pre-war have said that a different man returned. For example, Elsie Edwards remembered being engaged to her husband-to-be and finding it difficult to cope with his mood swings on his return.

Harold Wade remembers finding it difficult to adapt and fortunately having a good boss who, though not a serviceman himself, made allowances. Harold remembers having to dig tunnels when he was a POW but not knowing why.

This is a personal message from

H.Q. ALFSEA

to all newly-released Allied Prisoners of War.

"YOU ARE NEWS NOW AND ANYTHING YOU SAY IN PUBLIC OR TO PRESS REPORTERS IS LIABLE TO BE PUBLISHED IN THE PRESS OF THE WHOLE WORLD. YOU WILL HAVE DIRECT OR INDIRECT KNOWLEDGE OF THE FATE OF MANY OF YOUR COMRADES WHO DIED IN ENEMY HANDS AS A RESULT OF BRUTALITY OR NEGLECT. YOUR STORY IF PUBLISHED IN THE MORE LURID AND SENSA - TIONAL PRESS WILL CAUSE MUCH UNNECESSARY UNHAPPINESS TO RELATIVES AND FRIENDS. IF YOU HAVE NOT BEEN LUCKY ENOUGH TO HAVE BEEN RECOVERED AND HAD DIED ANY FORM OF UNPLEASANT DEATH AT THE HANDS OF THE JAPANESE YOU WOULD NOT HAVE WISHED YOUR FAMILY AND FRIENDS TO HAVE BEEN HARROWED BY LURID DETAILS OF THAT DEATH IN THE SENSATIONAL PRESS. THAT IS JUST WHAT WILL HAPPEN TO THE FAMILIES OF YOUR COMRADES WHO DIED IN THAT WAY IF YOU START TALKING TO ALL AND SUNDRY ABOUT YOUR EXPERIENCES. IT IS FELT CERTAIN THAT NOW YOU KNOW THE REASON FOR THIS ORDER YOU WILL TAKE PAINS TO SPARE THE FEELINGS OF OTHERS. ARRANGE- MENTS HAVE BEEN MADE FOR YOU TO TELL YOUR STORY TO INTERROGATING OFFICERS WHO WILL GET YOU TO WRITE IT DOWN YOU ARE NOT TO SAY ANYTHING TO ANYONE UNTIL AFTER YOU HAVE WRITTEN OUT YOUR STATEMENT AND HANDED IT IN.

2MFS/E/I

Maurice Naylor's account gives a very clear insight into how he felt on his return.

I found the next few weeks very distressing. Naturally my immediate family were overjoyed to see me home, but apart from them I got the impression that generally most people were indifferent or uninterested in what had gone on in the Far East.

There seemed to be a conspiracy of silence. People seemed to be embarrassed when they learnt I had been a prisoner in the Far East and changed the conversation. Whether this was out of consideration for me or for other reasons I do not know for sure. I believe the authorities had warned relatives not to ask questions.

There was no recognition of post-traumatic stress disorder then, and people were themselves unsure of what they were suffering. As Maurice says, *"I decided that the problem was with me. I found I could no longer socialise. I had recurrent nightmares about still being in captivity. I could not bear to listen to trivial conversations that went on, the grumbles about rations, the difficulties in getting furniture, the hundred and one petty irritations that were common in the aftermath of six years of war.*

Many a time I fled to the privacy of my bedroom and burst into tears. My family must have had a difficult time with me. None of this was unique to me and I sympathise with the parents, wives, children and grandchildren of former FEPOWs who had to cope with "a stranger in the house".

Maurice arrived home in time for his 25th birthday and eventually went back to his old job, later marrying and having children of his own. (Naylor, 2012) But for many, after such a long time away, there were sometimes more personal problems to deal with – a wife remarrying if he had been reported missing in action, or in some cases wives and girlfriends jilting them while they were away, often in favour of American soldiers based in Britain during the war.

Dr Bill Frankland, who had been a POW, sent me these details to include here:
I am sending you my very early post war memory.
In 1946 for some unknown reason I developed a very itchy generalised urticaria. It kept me awake at night as I scratched myself. As a Doctor I had much to learn about new treatments. We had never heard about antihistamine drugs or penicillin.

I must try the antihistamine Phenergan for my complaint. I had no Doctor to write out the necessary prescription but I thought I would be able to obtain the tablets from the local pharmacy. I went to see them and told them I could write out a prescription if necessary. The Pharmacist would not agree. How did he know that I was a Doctor? I told him I was wearing an RAMC (Royal Army Medical Corps) tie. He told me that this was not helpful. I might be a quarter master and therefore non-medical. He was a foreigner (by his accent) but very knowledgeable and he was telling me what I feared - was I knowledgeable enough after a gap of three and a half years to know enough medicine to be called a Doctor.

Three days later my brother-in-law Dr. John Ryle - ex navy, had come to congratulate my wife, ex Navy, for her recent decoration. He heard my story and like me was furious. He said that he would come with me to the Pharmacy and if I could not get my tablets, he would give the Pharmacist a piece of his mind. We went to the Pharmacy and for some reason without any questions I was given the necessary tablets which quite incidentally dealt with my complaint.

Another FEPOW, Govan Easton, remembered: *When we returned to Liverpool in 1945, the revenue checked all POW as they left the ship in case they had exceeded the 200 cigarette allowance. Some had to pay or have cigs confiscated. I was a casualty and taken off by Red Cross so I avoided this check!*

Another child of a FEPOW was sad to say: *I was born at the time my father was on his way to Singapore and he died almost two years later in July 1943 of cardiac beri beri at Chungkai military base hospital, so I never knew him at all*

An example of the lack of understanding by the authorities in Britain is a story in the 2002 COFEPOW Newsletter that says it all!

Martin [Prechner] tells me that when his father (a POW in Singapore and Java) was demobbed in 1946, he received a bill from the Royal Air Force for £1.18s. When he queried this he was told it was the cost of the greatcoat he did not return after the war (Editor, 2002).

THE COST OF CAPTIVITY

If you were to ask any POW what price did he pay for his 3½ years of captivity in a Japanese camp, I doubt if you would get a direct answer - there just isn't one - or is there?

They paid high, those young men, thousands paid the ultimate price. Those who returned paid the price of never being able to forget the starvation, horrifying diseases, watching their friends and comrades die and being ridiculed, humiliated and beaten.

To-day, we would like to think that when they returned they were offered the best. The best of care and attention, the best hospital treatment, the best counselling and the best of everything because they deserved it - they had paid for it. But sadly this was not the case.
There ill treatment and suffering was never recognised and this could not be illustrated more so than by a letter I recently received from one of our members, Martin Prechner.

Martin tells me that when his father (a POW in Singapore and Java) was demobbed in 1946, he received a bill from the Royal Air Force for £1.18s. When he queried this he was told it was the cost of the greatcoat he did not return after the war. Copy of a letter shown.

This really defies belief and once again demonstrates that the powers -to -be had absolutely no idea of what went on out there - perhaps he should have handed in his "jap-happy" which he most probably swapped his great coat for.

ROYAL AIR FORCE.

From :— No. 104 P.D.C., R.A.F., Hednesford.

To :— 1223415 AC Prechner, M., 7 Cloister Gardens, EDGWARE, Middlesex.

Date :— 5th March, 1946.

Ref :— 104 PDC/171/11/P/Q/Accts.

STATEMENT OF ACCOUNT.

With reference to your letter dated 13th February, 1946, the charge of £1 18s. 0d. is in respect of a greatcoat not returned at the time of release.

P/O.
(J. H. MICHELLS),
for Group Captain, Commanding,
No. 104 P.D.C., R.A.F., Hednesford.

The following notes relate to Captain Kenneth Mitchell Hughes of The Manchester Regiment and Royal Artillery who, sadly, did not come home from the Far East.

I am attaching copies of the last letters written by my husband's uncle upon his release from captivity in August 1945. The originals have been 'lost' so these are typewritten copies that were sent to members of his family. Regrettably, his diary was never found so the content of these letters are the only details we have of his time spent as a prisoner. On admission to hospital in Rangoon [we have still not been able to identify the hospital], he will have been incubating Scrub Typhus and without appropriate medication and low resistance, he could not combat the onset of the disease and sadly died. He was aged 32 years. This news came as a huge blow to his parents. My husband, as an 8 year old, remembers the day the telegram arrived, he was despatched to another room whilst the enormity of the news was read and absorbed.

There is an irony to this story - as a young man, Ken loved model railways and had a wonderful collection. Little did any one realise that within a few years he would be working on the most notorious of railways and one which would bring about his premature death.

C O P Y 3rd. letter received 21/9/45. ex P.O.W. AIR MAIL.

9th September 1945.

My dear Mother & Father,

This is the third letter I have written since the end of the war and I am still in an ex P.O.W. Camp in Thailand at a place called Pratchai about 80 miles North of Bangkok. In case the other 2 letters do not reach you this will more or less be a repeat of my earlier letters. I have just heard that I am to leave this Camp to-morrow morning at 11 o'clock by road for Bangkok from where we shall fly to Rangoon, so at last I feel I am on my way home. Well, how are you both, and all the members of the family? I am longing to get into touch with you once more as my last postcard from you was dated June 1944 - over 15 months ago. As soon as I can I shall let you know by cable an address to which you can cable and write me a long letter.

Briefly, what has happened to me since the fall of Singapore is as follows:-

At the end of the battle all P.O.W.'s. were concentrated in Changi. 6 weeks later I was on the first party of prisoners to leave Malaya. Our destination turned out to be Saigon in French-Indo-China. Where we arrived 6 days later, having travelled by sea in an overcrowded Japanese freighter. The party consisted of 1,000 other Ranks and 30 Officers, including a number of Officers and men from my own unit, so I have been with some great friends of mine throughout my P.O.W. existence. We were employed on Dock Labouring at Saigon where we stayed until June 1943. Conditions at Saigon were'nt too bad, and the local French European population were very helpful indeed - secretly giving us Medical supplies, &c. Then in June 1943 700 of us were moved to Thailand to build the railway connecting Bangkok with Burma. We travelled by river boat to Puom Pengh, Capital of Cambodia, where we continued our journey by rail via Bangkok to the Burma frontier. Then, for 6 months, we endured the most terrible of conditions living in jungle camps where thousands of P.O.W.'s died from dysentry, malaria, cholera, malnutrition etc. Early in 1944 we came down to camps on the plain near Bangkok where conditions improved. Since then I have been in 4 different camps until I find myself here. Officers were segregated from other Ranks in January of this year. You will be glad to hear that I am now in excellent health. I have lost a lot of weight which is only to be expected, now weighing just over 9st. instead of my normal 11½st. but I think by the time I get home I shall be back to normal again. My only illness has been malaria from which I suffered for 14 months, getting attacks every two or three weeks but I am glad to say that I have been free from it since February of this year. But now, thanks to God, this miserable existence is all over and I have got the good things to look forward to - The greatest moment of my life will be when I return home to you at 8 Kensington Gardens.

Continued -

Harry Stogden was instrumental in making the Changi Cross referred to earlier. He was a POW in Changi for the first part of his captivity, then went to Fukuoka in Japan working in the coal mines. He was constantly in and out of hospital and wrote several letters to his wife, Phyllis, not knowing that she had died from pneumonia a year after he left the UK.

He told her of his plans for when he returned, of the house he wanted to find for them to live in as a family, unaware that two of his small children were now in the care of their grandmother and the youngest daughter now living with his own sister. It was a while before he received a letter from his mother-in-law telling him of his wife's death, and although he was on his way home on the hospital ship, he died suddenly and was buried at sea. (Cordingly L. , 2015)

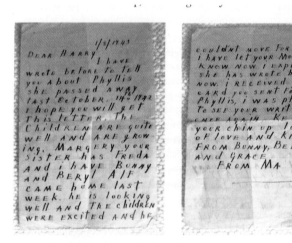

Harry's mother-in-law had to write this poignant letter to him.

I do hope to be with you soon and I do want to love and care for my wife and our children as I have never done before. I always think of you in my prayers trusting that God will look after you all.

April 15th 43

Well dear, here I am again, have been in hospital [Roberts Hospital)] for a few weeks with a little stomach trouble but am getting along quite well now. I have been dreaming about you and the children for many nights now and I wonder sometimes if you dream of me. Sometimes they are nice dreams, sometimes not quite so nice. Many of the troops have been moved away up country, many more are going in a few days' time. I still remain behind; just where I shall finish up I don't know. How are things with you now, hope you are not worrying too much. You must excuse this writing as this is an awful pen and ink, still it is better than none, (I shall have to write single pages now as the ink goes right through).

Good Friday April 23rd 43.

Am still in the hospital, this is the 8th week, have had "Diarrhoea" but rid of that now but have got painful feet, all due to poor food. However we must trust good fortune. More troops are going away this week-end; don't know where they are going to.

Today is Easter Sunday 1943

To-day dear I think I will tell you my plans for the future. After my discharge the first thing I would like to do is to take you and the children for a holiday to somewhere, anyway there is a holiday for you and me. Well then the next thing is for me to find a job. ...I would like to go away from London to the provincial districts, you know – near the country but not too far from the town, somewhere where houses are cheaper, also rents and the cost of living, but I would like to discuss this with you. ...I think there will be plenty of jobs in my line as there will be plenty of work after the war.

Well after that comes the question of finding a house, the most difficult job of all but never mind. When we have found one I have big ideas of Electricity.

When British women were repatriated, the Home Office asked relatives and friends not to meet ships when they docked, there was no formal welcome back or press coverage and L Warner (Warner, 1982) refers to *"the shame-faced public attitude of the authorities towards these war victims"*. Just as sad is the fact that the War Graves Commission has scant records of women who died as Far East civilian internees.

There was no central fund to help the women. When they were released from the various camps, the Red Cross provided warm clothing to prepare them for the climate back home in Britain. On arrival, they were also given some extra clothing coupons as they had left their homes and belongings behind when they were captured, although British shop owners apparently had very negative views about why they should get these coupons!

The claim process for ex-POWs was announced in a newspaper advertisement saying they all had to apply in writing to the Colonial Office to receive a standard payment of £35. For the women who were interned, they found it difficult to resume a normal family life, as did the FEPOW men of course, particularly as they had become so resourceful and independent during their captivity.

While many ex-FEPOWs refer to the lack of help from the government and the general lack of understanding from people, this situation was not confined to Britain.

For example, Pat Aspromourgos describes the situation in Australia where they were sent in 1940.

We didn't really receive any help or support here in Australia. Money was very short. We had rationing here but not as severe as in England. Some parts of Australia were bombed, but a long way away from where we were.

We were called names at school, and when people heard our [English] accents they would say "why don't you pommies go back to where you came from?" After the war, because my father had been killed, my mother decided not to return to England. She felt she had no reason to go back and that there could be more opportunities for us growing up here. At that time, there were three of us children with my brother and younger sister.

Pat married and continued to live in Australia. However, as a last note, she says *"I am afraid I still remember the treatment we received when we came here sorely in need of love and assistance"*. So, as we know, some memories stay with us for a very long time, whether we want them to or not.

Wherever prisoners were held in the Far East, and irrespective of the length of time they were POWs, all research shows that the impact was the same. If they had been away for several years, wives or girlfriends would have been involved in the war effort at home, often experiencing more independence than ever before. Needless to say, this changed the relationship between couples considerably, especially if the former FEPOW now needed substantial care to help recovery from physical or psychological wounds.

There are many examples of recurring nightmares and shouting in the night. I was born in 1948, and always just remember my father as a happy, funny man who was quiet and unassuming. There are things I realise now would have been very difficult for him – when I was in primary school, we had a supply teacher who was Japanese and taught us how to say 'good morning' in Japanese. I was so proud of being able to repeat this at home, yet he said nothing to make me feel bad about it.

When we had to go to hospital with my little brother, Dad fainted in the waiting area as they wheeled someone past with lots of blood on the covers. Often, the attitude to food changed, with an urgency to make sure every scrap of food was eaten and not wasted, more so in the early years when rationing was still in force.

Ex-British PoWs fight for torture cash

by Hedda Archbold

EMPEROR Hirohito's remains were laid to rest in Tokyo on Friday. But for the British soldiers who suffered in Japanese PoW camps, hostilities have still not ceased.

The Japanese Labour Camp Survivors' Association is fighting to get compensation for the hardship and torture endured during their imprisonment by the Japanese.

On their return to Britain, survivors were awarded the Burma Star, as a compensation for all they endured for King and country.

Following the Japanese Peace Treaty Settlement, each soldier was awarded a paltry £3 compensation. Five years later, they received another £76.40 from the Government who sold frozen Japanese assets in Britain: a pittance at any rate, especially considering that Japanese citizens interned in Canada and the US during wartime received $20,000 each for "inconvenience caused".

However, when Hirohito visited the Queen in 1971 he was made Knight of the Garter, the highest order of chivalry.

"We didn't demonstrate against Hirohito's visit then because the authorities had asked us not to, in order to save our Queen embarrassment," said Mr Fred Eva, one of the survivors.

"We have great respect for our Royal Family, so we complied with their wish." Many of them did, however, send back their medals, saying that their decorations did not mean anything to them any more.

The storm of protest that arose over Prince Philip's attendance at the funeral was met by those same authorities with raised eyebrows. Why on earth kick up a fuss now when you didn't seem to mind when the man came here 18 years ago?

The Far East PoW Association organised commemorative services all over Britain last Friday to honour their 12,433 comrades who died in the prison camps.

But the Japanese Labour Camp Survivors Association, chaired by Mr Bill Holtham, wants to take matters a step further than peaceful protest and is claiming £10,000 for each survivor from the Japanese government.

The issue has been brought before the Human Rights Court by Canadian ex-PoWs. British, Australian and New Zealand veterans are waiting for the verdict which will set a precedent for thousands like them.

Not all Far East PoWs agree with the claim. Mr Harold Payne of the Far East PoW Association feels the Peace Treaty settled their compensation. Mr Holtham sneers at that. "Of course that lot aren't on our side; they've all got OBEs and MBEs. That's why they don't want to rock the boat."

When Mr Eva saw Prince Philip bow to Emperor Akihito, he felt the ground disappear from under his feet; "The Japs said 45 years ago: 'We might have lost this war, but we'll rule the world in a 100 years.' Philip doesn't realise the war is still going on."

More than 50,000 British soldiers were taken captive in the 1939-45 War by the Japanese, who had never before taken prisoners-of-war. The Japanese code of honour makes every soldier duty bound to fight to the end, and die rather than capitulate. Consequently they treated their prisoners-of-war with utter contempt and almost offhand cruelty.

PoWs were bundled into cattle trucks — 30 a truck — and taken to the edge of the jungle, a continuous journey lasting five days. They were marched through more than 200 miles of virgin jungle, to reach the area where they were made to build their own prison camps.

They were set to work in the mines in the area as well as on the railway line along the river Kwai.

All possessions were taken from them. All they were left with was a loincloth, which most of them wore for the three years of hard labour that followed.

They worked from dawn till well after dark, sustained on a diet of rice and "stew" (water with slivers of marrow). Many died of malnutrition. Most of the survivors came out weighing no more than 7 st.

There was little or no medical care. Those who suffered dysentery, malaria, beri beri, cholera or tropical ulcers were left to die. The £70,000 worth of Red Cross parcels sent never reached the prisoners.

All prisoners had to bow to their captors, who saw themselves as representatives of the Emperor. If they didn't bow low enough, says Mr Harold Payne, President of the Far East PoW Association, they would be beaten with a stick, a bayonet or anything to hand.

The recent disclosure of Australian archive material has reminded everyone how cruel and widespread were Japanese war crimes, including, for instance, the use of prisoners as guinea pigs in germ warfare experiments, and cannibalism in the camps.

Hard labour: British PoWs working for the Japanese

6. Reconciliation

The first question must be "what does this actually mean?"

As an individual, it is not easy to come to terms with everything that happened, especially when so much of the ill-treatment was unnecessarily cruel. Typically, nightmares, angry outbursts or bouts of depression, and reliving the torment, persist for many years. While modern thinking on trauma suggests counselling is a major factor in recovery, this was not an option in post-war Britain. As many former POWs say, you just got on with it the best you could.

Even if you find a way to reconcile these experiences and where you are today, this does not mean you forget them. Perhaps as a Christian (or believer in whichever God you choose), you can find the courage to forgive if not forget. For example, when film-maker Akinori (referred to earlier) was putting his documentary together and interviewing people, Mr Cyril Ramsey could not bring himself to be in the same photograph with him or shake his hand (Macaulay, 2001).

For him, reconciliation means he is glad that Akinori is making the film so that younger generations of Japanese fully grasp the enormity of what happened and the actions taken by their own people. As another FEPOW says, he still hates Japan, but accepts that later generations are not to blame and should know the truth.

The question of reconciliation is broader than the feelings of the individual. For many, recognition of what happened in the camps is a starting point, but is there an official apology? Definitely an emotive topic!

Before Hirohito's visit to Britain, there were calls for a formal apology to be given. There was indeed a lack-lustre suggestion of an apology, yet many felt it was just a token gesture in order to smooth the path for the visit.

The death of Emperor Hirohito in 1989 was a significant event, not least because it signalled the end of the regime directly responsible for the war actions of the Japanese in the Far East during WWII.

However, there were considerable repercussions around the staging of his funeral and the international response to this by sending high-level representatives. The attendance of Prince Philip as representative of our monarchy, and Sir Geoffrey Howe as our political representative resulted in a reawakening of anger and was seen as "a slap in the face" by many who had suffered as FEPOWs (Wyllie a. , 1989).

The Sun newspaper was particularly concerned and editorial comment was especially scathing, suggesting Sir Howe ask questions of the new Japanese Premier about a recent speech. Mr Takeshita had "refused to admit that Japan was an aggressor in the last war" and that it was for future historians to decide on the truth (Editor, 1989).

They devoted several pages to events in Japan at the time of the funeral, including coverage of offensive anti-Queen slogans on the side of a dustcart as Prince Philip arrived in Japan, and the fact that he made only a token gesture of a nod to the coffin – considered a bit of an insult but his presence there at all gave them some form of 'moral victory' (Arnold, Japs jibe at Queen, 1989) (Arnold, We are nod amused, 1989).

At the same time, there were many services being held across Britain to remember those who died, or were held in captivity, under Hirohito's rule. In Poole, veterans of WWII gathered in protest supported by the Mayor and Sherriff of Poole (Old comrades in protest, 1989) and in Weymouth, hundreds of ex-POWs marched to the Cenotaph in protest at sending the Duke of Edinburgh to Hirohito's funeral. Evidence had emerged earlier that Hirohito had in fact ordered that prisoners of war were to be killed if Japan was invaded (Wyllie A. , 1989).

This funeral certainly illustrated how FEPOWs, their families and even those with no direct connection to the hostilities, were dismayed at the way someone directly responsible for the suffering and death of so many should be honoured so publicly (Maslin, 1989).

It was also noted, by John Anderson of the Burma Star Association (Sunday Express April 1989), how attendance at this funeral was a completely different official decision compared with the refusal to send any member of the Royal family to the funeral of Empress Zita of Austria due to the presence of Kurt Waldheim, a known supporter of the Nazi regime.

Whether they were in favour of some form of reconciliation, forgetting the past was an insult to the many who could still remember the atrocities carried out and individual fallen comrades. These sentiments were not just expressed by British FEPOWs, but also by many Americans who had their own memories of the war and expressed their anger at George Bush for attending Hirohito's funeral (O'Sullivan).

Compensation

While working as FEPOW secretary, I was directly involved with the fight for compensation. It took 50 years for the government to actually agree to pay the sadly-depleted numbers of POWs still alive, decades later than compensation payments were agreed and paid to German POWs for instance. Even when it was finally agreed, there were still individuals who had delays while trying to convince officials they actually were in prison camps given the lack of accurate records. You might think their medical records would demonstrate exactly how they spent their war years.

After the end of WWII, various treaties were signed and formal agreements made to compensate prisoners of war. In fact, those who were captured in Europe fared much better than those imprisoned in harsher labour camps of the Far East as Germany was willing to accept its responsibilities.

After the treaty was signed with the Japanese, FEPOWs received £3 compensation with a further payment of £76.40 as the British government sold off seized Japanese assets. This was in stark contrast to the $20,000 received by Japanese who had been interned in Canada and America! (Archbold, 1989)

Dorset POWs join in compensation battle

By Belinda Ryan

SOUTH Dorset ex-prisoners of war who suffered horrific treatment in Japanese labour camps are still fighting for compensation.

And tomorrow a group of about 25 members of the South Dorset branch of the Japanese Labour Camp Survivors' Association will be meeting up with fellow members from all over the country at the House of Commons to lobby MPs.

For all of them, the suffering they endured more than 40 years ago still preys on their minds.

Mr. Gordon Pearman (71), of Wentworth Close, Weymouth, was a prisoner in more than ten camps in Singapore, Thailand and Saigon over three and a half years.

He said: "We want it recognised that the Japanese are responsible for the hell we went through. People now couldn't possi-bly understand the physi-cal and mental strain we were under.

"Murder, beating, lack of medical facilities and no clothes were common place."

Mr. Pearman believes he was one of the lucky ones because he came back after the war. But he said for several years after he had terrible nightmares.

"The past 40 years have been 40 bonus years," he said. "I think the majority of us who survived feel that way.

"But many who came back died within ten years — I suppose they could not live with it."

And Mr Pearson said the prisoners were stripped of all dignity. He said they were not given clothes after their own uniforms were out and he had no shoes for two years.

"When I went to work building the Thai to Burma Railway I worked 20 hours a day in condi-tions which are indescri-bable," he said. "We were working up to our knees in mud doing navvying.

"My normal weight then was ten stone and I dropped down to about eight. One chap, who had been a champion cycle road racer, was usually 11st. 11lb. and he went down to six and a half stone."

Mr. Pearman said that no amount of misery could ever compensate for the atrocities suffered by him-self and fellow prisoners of war.

But all of them — and their families — deserve something.

"My wife Edith went through hell too — not knowing whether she was a wife or a widow," he said.

The former prisoners are asking for a total of £4,000 each from the Japanese Government. The figure is very close to the claim of 10,000 dollars the Canadians are making against the Japanese — although the amounts were decided independent-ly and the fact they are so close is purely coinciden-tal.

Mr. Pearman said: "That works out at about £6 for each day I spent in a labour camp."

And he hopes this claim will win the support of the MPs.

"All the Dorset MPs have been contacted and they all seem to be very sympathetic to our cause. We're hoping they will back us."

There was growing pressure from FEPOWs to claim compensation and 1988 saw a more concerted effort to get MPs on board. While many FEPOW associations around the UK were involved, South Dorset Association was particularly vocal with the support of their MP Mr Ian Bruce. There was editorial comment in Dorset Evening Echo and several articles outlining why the claims were being brought (Editor, 1988) (Ryan, Dorset POWs join in compensation battle, 1988) (Ryan, MP backs POW's cash campaign, 1988).

All-party support for Bruce's PoW fight

MPs from all parties have supported South Dorset MP Mr. Ian Bruce in his fight to win compensation for former prisoners of war who were held by the Japanese.

And, as yesterday saw the 43rd anniversary of VJ Day, Mr. Bruce said he was very close to reaching his target of 200 signatures for his all-party early day motion.

The Conservative MP put forward the motion to ensure the matter was discussed in the House of commons. It received great support from fellow Conservative Sir Bernard Braine who spoke on the issue in the House and other sponsors include former Labour leader Michael Foot and Labour's former Home

and Northern Ireland Secretary, Merlyn Reece.

The motion states: "That this House, in welcoming the growing friendship between Japan and the United Kingdom, believes that this friendship will not fully blossom until the wrongs done during the Second World War to Allied prisoners are fully accepted by the Japanese Government and due reparation made."

Figures available shortly before Parliament's summer recess showed that 176 MPs had signed the document.

Mr. Bruce said: "I was hoping at least 200 MPs would sign. I'm not quite sure what the exact figure is at the moment because people can still sign during the recess but I know another 12 can be added to the total."

MP backs POW's cash campaign

ECHO MAY 16 88

By Belinda Ryan

SOUTH Dorset MP Ian Bruce is to call for a debate in the House of Commons on compensation for Japanese labour camp survivors.

His move follows a meeting with members of the South Dorset branch of the Japanese Labour Camp Survivors Association who were among a group of about 1,000 ex-prisoners who travelled to London from all over

the country to lobby their MPs.

The former prisoners are demanding compensation for themselves for the horrific treatment and cruelty they endured at the hands of their Japanese jailers and also for the families of the men who were murdered by the Japanese guards and soldiers.

Mr. Bruce presented a letter detailing the demands of the Japanese Labour Camp Survivors Association, to Mr. Akio Suda, a political councillor at the Japanese Embassy. The letter will be sent directly to the Japanese prime minister Mr. Noboru Takeshita.

Mr. Bruce said: "We got Mr. Suda to acknowledge that clearly an injustice

had been done and we said that we want this to be looked at at the very

And Mr. Bruce said he would be putting forward a motion to ensure attention was drawn to the matter in the House of Commons.

He added: "I'm going to put forward an Early Day Motion. I want it seen that the Japanese do have a responsibility to these people."

Mr. Godson Pearman and Mr. Ron Mould both travelled from Weymouth to the House of Commons to speak to Mr. Bruce.

They were detained in Japanese labour camps for more than two years.

"We're fighting for compensation for the hell they put us through," said Mr. Pearman.

Mr. Mould said: "They are now a wealthy nation and we should be compensated."

But a Weymouth woman, whose uncle was murdered by the Japanese, said many British families had lost relatives and those families should receive compensation as well as the survivors.

Mr. Pearman stressed that although the organisation was called the Survivors Association they were in fact also campaigning for reparation to be made to relative of those killed.

And Mr. Bruce commented: "In everything these people do they always emphasise the widows and they want to see everyone compensated.

"In fact if anything they feel almost guilty they survived and so many of their comrades did not."

By 1989, when Hirohito's funeral took place, ex-prisoners of war were still trying to get compensation, although there was not always full support for this pressure (Archbold, 1989). Even Dame Vera Lynn entered the fray with a letter to the Sun newspaper deploring the cost of Hirohito's funeral (quoted as £46 million) compared with lack of financial support for veterans.

Help Jap victims

JAPANESE Emperor Hirohito's funeral is said to have cost £46million.

By contrast, Allied prisoners of war or their widows received £76 each under the terms of the Peace Treaty from Japan for their three-and-a-half years of barbarous treatment in captivity.

Members of the Burma Star Association, who fought in Burma, are very concerned that their comrades and the civilian internees who suffered, and the widows of those who died, will receive all the assistance they need. The Association's members have therefore launched a national appeal and will be grateful if members of the public will send whatever they can, however small, to the Far East Prisoners of War Central Welfare Fund, 30 Copsewood Way, Bearstead, Maidstone, Kent ME15 8PL.

The fund provides immediate assistance in cases of necessity and other help to all former men and women Far East prisoners of war and civilian internees. It is in urgent need of funds to continue its work.

DAME VERA: Cash plea

DAME VERA LYNN, Ditchling, W. Sussex

In July 1988 a Motion was brought to the House of Commons and graphically outlined why compensation should be paid (Holtham, 1988). It also referred to the actions of the Hong Kong Veterans of Canada who had taken a claim to the United Nations Human Rights Commission, and the fact that the Australian veterans will also be taking similar actions. These were compelling arguments.

Dear Members,

SIR BERNARD KEPT FAITH WITH HIS
PROMISE TO RAISE THE QUESTION OF COMPEN-
SATION AND TO DRAW ATTENTION TO THE SPLE-
NDID CANADIAN IMAGINATIVE INITIATIVE TO
TAKE THE COMPLAINT TO THE UNITED NATIONS.

JERRY COX, OUR INTELLIGENCE OFFICER
FROM WEYMOUTH WAS A FOUNDER MEMBER OF
JLCSA AND FOUGHT CEASELESSLY TO SECURE
JUSTICE AND COMPENSATION FOR ALL FEPOWs.
HAND IN HAND WITH JEAN, HIS DEAR WIFE,
AND WITH HER DEEP UNSTANDING OF THE
JAPANESE AND THEIR LANGUAGE THEY FORMED
AN INDOMITABLE TEAM.   IT IS IRONIC THAT
ON THE DAY BEFORE JERRY PASSED TO HIGHER
SERVICE HE WAS AWARDED A 100% WAR
DISABILITY PENSION.

FRIENDS, IT IS WITH HUMILITY AND PRIDE,
AND ON YOUR BEHALF, I WOULD LIKE TO DEDICATE
SIR BERNARD'S SPEECH TO JERRY COX - A
LOYAL AND GALLANT GENTLEMAN.

Bill Holtham

Prisoners of War (Compensation)

Motion made, and Question proposed, That this House
do now adjourn.—[*Mr. Peter Lloyd.*]

10.40 pm

Sir Bernard Braine (Castle Point): I begin by drawing
the attention of my hon. and learned Friend the Minister
of State, Foreign and Commonwealth Office to all-party
early-day motion 119 in the name of my hon. Friend the
Member for Dorset, South (Mr. Bruce) which has now
attracted 176 signatures and which will, I promise, attract
a great deal more. The motion summarises succinctly what
I am about to say. It states:

That this House, in welcoming the growing friendship
between Japan and the United Kingdom, believes that this
friendship will not fully blossom until the wrongs done during
the Second World War to Allied prisoners are fully accepted
by the Japanese Government and due reparation made.

In 1941, at a moment of great peril for our country,
locked as we were in dealy conflict with Nazi Germany, the
Japanese struck suddenly and without warning at the
Americans, the Dutch and ourselves in the Pacific. By the
time Singapore had fallen, over 50,000 British service men
and women and civilians, 20,000 Australians and 1,700
Canadians who had defended Hong Kong with great
gallantry had fallen into enemy hands. Such was the
appalling treatment of these helpless prisoners that over a
quarter of them were either to be slaughtered in cold blood
or to die of disease, malnutrition and unbelievable
brutality by the time the Japanese surrendered.

I was a member of the personal staff of the Supreme
Allied Commander in South East Asia Admiral Lord
Mountbatten. I was in Asia in 1945 when the Japanese
surrendered. I was moved to tears by the first sight of the
pitiful survivors who came out from the hell of Japanese
captivity. Many of them, still in their 20s, were to die
prematurely, many more were disabled and crippled for
life.

It is difficult at this distance of time to describe what
they had endured. Field Marshal Slim, one of our greatest
soliders, has put on record what the victorious British 14th
Army found as it over ran the prison camps. He wrote:

"The state of these camps and of their wretched inmates
can only be realised by those who saw them as they were at
this time. Except for derelict huts and bashas, the camps were
little more than barbed wire enclosures in which wild beasts
might have been herded together. The Japanese and Korean
gaolers, almost without exception, were at the best callously
indifferent to suffering, or at the worst, bestially sadistic. The
food was of a quality and a quantity barely enough to keep
men alive, let alone fit them for the hard labour that most
were driven to perform. It was horrifying to see them moving
slowly about these sordid camps, all emaciated, many walking
skeletons, numbers covered with suppurating sores, and most
naked but for the ragged shorts they had worn for years or
loin cloths of sacking. The most heart-moving of all were
those who lay on wretched pallets, their strength ebbing faster
than relief could be brought to them."

He concluded:

"There can be no excuse for a nation which as a matter of
policy treats its prisoners of war in this way, and no honour
for any army, however brave, which willingly makes itself the
instrument of such inhumanity to the helpless".

I will mention just one case— I could mention a
thousand—recounted to me by a former prisoner who
suffered greatly. He refers to what happened to one of his
comrades in Sonkrai camp on the notorious Siam-Burma
railway. He said:

"He was chained to the teak tree at the entrance of the
camp and we had to pass him every dawn when going out to

In 1997, we were still fighting for compensation with Robin Cook pressing Japan for cash to compensate British prisoners (Harris, 1997). Crucially, all these efforts had been prolonged and FEPOW numbers were dwindling as they grew older and suffered long-term effects of the many illnesses they succumbed to in captivity.

PAGE SIX   DORSET EVENING ECHO Thursda

DORSET EVENING ECHO COMMENT

What price suffering ?

A LONG campaign to win compensation for former soldiers who were imprisoned in Japanese labour camps takes another step today.

Twenty-five members of the South Dorset branch of the Japanese Labour Camp Survivors' Association are meeting up with fellow members from all over the country to lobby MPs at the House of Commons.

The former prisoners-of-war are asking for a total of £6,000 each from the Japanese Government in compensation for the horrific treatment they received in the camps.

The claim seems modest enough. "It works out at about £6 for each day I spent in a labour camp," said Mr. Gordon Pearman, aged 71, who was a prisoner in more than ten camps in Singapore, Thailand and Saigon over three-and-a-half years.

It is clear that the suffering the men endured more than 40 years ago still haunts them today.

Mr. Pearman said: "We want it recognised that the Japanese are responsible for the hell we went through. People now cannot possibly understand the physical and mental strain we were under."

The prisoners cannot erase the memories of horrific murders and beatings in the camps. They remember how meagre the medical facilities were and how they were frequently left without clothes.

We can well understand why they intend to pursue their claim relentlessly. As Mr. Pearman says, no amount of money could ever compensate for the atrocities suffered by the prisoners, but all of them — and their families — deserve something.

Let's hope the men are able to win the support of their MPs to back their case. They have had to, wait far too long already for their compensation.

Cook shows the way

THOUGH the war with Japan has been over for more than fifty years, some memories can never fade. For the 12,000 surviving Britons who were starved and tortured in the barbarity of the labour camps, those memories are all the more bitter because they never received proper compensation.

Today there is some hope. Foreign Secretary Robin Cook intends to press the issue when he meets his Japanese counterpart in London. It makes a welcome change from the last few months of Tory rule, when the Foreign Office tamely gave up the fight.

Traditionally, it used to be the Tories who looked after the men and women who fought for their country. Yet they showed little sympathy to victims of Gulf War Syndrome. They gave up the battle for the PoWs. How piquant that on both issues it has taken Labour to remind us of proper Conservative values.

In fact, the COFEPOW newsletter of 1999 printed an article from The Canadian Press that surviving FEPOWs were each awarded $24,000 tax free, based on $18 per day of imprisonment (Ward, 1999). It should be noted that this was in relation to forced labour of POWs not "compensation for captivity", and also that it came from the Canadian government not Japan.

There were lots of suggestions of what this compensation should be, but one FEPOW (Mr Gordon Pearman) said that a sum of £6000 represented £6 for each day he worked in the 10 different labour camps across Singapore, Saigon and Thailand. Not an unreasonable sum and certainly comparable with what others had received.

The biggest stumbling block was always Japan's refusal to recognise that they had any obligations to compensate prisoners given the Treaty they signed in 1951. As with all things legal, it depended how you interpreted the jargon!

Another argument was that Japan said they never paid any other compensation than that agreed at the time. However, a book published in 1993 (Matthews, 1993) included documents passed between Swiss banks and the Japanese Foreign Office. These showed that in order to access their funds held in Swiss banks, the Japanese were obliged to pay compensation to the relatives of Swiss nationals murdered during the siege of Manila.

Interestingly, they paid a million Swiss francs as compensation to the 13 families, and actually stated in writing that they agreed this compensation "was justified"

(Stubbs, 1997). We were successful, finally, in receiving compensation and ultimately a belated apology from Japan for the inhumane way all FEPOWs were treated during captivity.

In the end, British FEPOWs received an ex-gracia payment of £10,000 with the help of pressure from Royal British Legion. Of course, by the year 2000, there were not so many FEPOWS or their spouses surviving, but at least it was a welcome recompense to those remaining.

Initiatives to encourage reconciliation

There have been many initiatives to encourage reconciliation, certainly since late 1980s (Holtham, 1989). Visits have been arranged for ex-FEPOWS and their families to return to the places where they were interned have been organised regularly.

Many of these have been funded through joint initiatives, including those of Royal British Legion, but also as personal pilgrimages such as those organised to River Kwai region by Peter Dunstan (he was instrumental in collating details of all British who died in the Far East). For example, Maurice Naylor went to Thailand on holiday in 1981 and made a special effort to visit the bridge over the River Kwai as well as the War Cemetery in Kanchanaburi (Naylor, 2012).

Postcard of River Kwai Bridge

Mrs Keiko Holmes is someone closely associated with such pilgrimages. Originally from Tokyo, she met her husband when studying at university and they moved to England. In the early 1990s, visiting her family at Itaya she found a memorial to British FEPOWs who had worked in the copper mine at Iruku. On her return to the UK she started what was to be a long-term quest to find ex-FEPOWs and organise visits to Japan and Thailand. I know my father talked of working in the copper mines, though he did not say where they were except that it was while he was in POW camp in Japan. (Stubbs, 1998).

Crucially, she has also done a great deal to make sure the Japanese people are aware of what happened to prisoners during captivity. Her visits were not always positively viewed by some FEPOWs, of course, as they felt that although she was "a very genuine person", she was being used by the Japanese government who funded most of the trips.

However, in 1997 Sadaaki Numata of the Anglo-Japanese Economic Institute presented a diplomat's impression of links between the two countries. He specifically refers to the Japanese Embassy's recognition of the positive work done by Mrs Holmes to help heal *"old wounds on the part of those who underwent tremendous pain and suffering" during the war in the Far East* (Numata, 1997). Whatever your personal feelings about whether reconciliation is truly possible, he was presenting a changed view of Japan's "resolve never to repeat the mistakes of the past".

Philip Malins MBE MC was involved in the release of prisoners when the Japanese finally surrendered. For many years, he was instrumental in organising trips to the Far East regions so that ex-FEPOWs and their families could perhaps find some personal closure to the events so long ago.

Remembrance Day November 1997

In 1997, I was asked to take part in a Reconciliation Visit to Japan, and to lay the wreath at the Remembrance Service at Hodogaya Commonwealth Cemetery in Yokohama. I was there to represent British FEPOWs as well as my father who had been captured in Hong Kong. There was a group of three generations on the trip – myself as daughter of a FEPOW, Mrs Karen Goodwin whose grand-father Gunner Emrys

Williams died in captivity aged just 38, and her 14 year old daughter Claire.

Karen's grandmother received a letter in January 1946 from the Commanding Officer at the Fukuoka camp where Emrys died. The camp where they were seemed to be better than others we have heard about, and although Emrys had been ill for a while, he had been getting better then suddenly died.

Captain Williams (not related) said that he had performed the funeral ceremony, and the ashes of all inmates there were finally handed to the Embarkation staff at the end of the war. He was not sure what would happen to them after that, but we were able to see Emrys' grave at the Cemetery, something Karen and her family had wanted to do for a long time.

GREAT-GRANDAD, I LOVE YOU

Claire's pilgrimage to Japan war grave

A MIDLAND schoolgirl will tomorrow make a pilgrimage to the Yokohama war grave of her great-grandfather at the invitation of the Japanese.

Fourteen-year-old Claire Thompson's great-grandfather Emrys Williams, of Hallam Street, West Bromwich, died in March 1945 in a Japanese slave-labour copper mine after being captured as a Royal Artillery gunner at Singapore.

Sixteen years ago Mr Williams' grand-daughter Karen Goodwin, aged 36, of Woodbourne Road, Smethwick, carried out research into his death.

She discovered that he died at the age of 38 in a copper mine near Nagasaki, Japan, from Bright's Disease, caused by a lack of clean drinking water.

by PETER SWINGLER

great-grandfather's grave."

Karen said: "I wrote to the War Graves Commission for more information and I received correspondence and help from the Midland Area of Far East Prisoners of War Associations.

"We then received an invitation from the Japanese government to attend the Hodogaya Wood Cemetery, where my grandfather is buried.

Wreath

Karen's daughter Claire will fly to Japan to lay a wreath at her great-grandfather's grave at Hodogaya Commonwealth War Cemetery, the only Commonwealth war cemetery in Japan.

She will be accompanied by a member of the Midland Far East Prisoners of War Associations.

Claire said: "I am interested in the Second World War. I am looking forward to placing a wreath on my great-grandfather's grave on Remembrance Day.

"The Japanese government is paying all costs involved for a week's stay and Claire said she would like to go and put a wreath on her

■ I WILL REMEMBER: Claire Thompson will lay a wreath on the grave in Japan of her great-grandfather Gunner Emrys Williams, top. Picture JOHN REAVENALL

The visit was arranged following a newspaper article about Claire wanting to visit her great-grandfather's grave. The British Embassy and staff had taken great care to locate Mr Williams' grave, so Karen and Claire were able to lay the wreaths they had brought specially.

It was a very formal occasion, with lots of international guests and all major religions represented.

I laid the wreath to remember those that returned and those that died in the camps.

This was reported on the front page of the newsletter of the Japanese Embassy in London ("Japan" No 643 25/11/97) and in a personal letter, they noted that the ceremony had been very moving and marked another step to reconciliation. Clearly, it was a significant gesture for everyone concerned.

We were very honoured, of course, and although my father was very ill at this time (he died a few months later in the following February) he was still very positive about the need for reconciliation (Japan Information & Cultural Centre (Embassy of Japan), 1997).

This is a beautiful setting, the cemetery and gardens designed and stocked through the efforts of Lt Col Len Harrop MBE. He arranged for trees and shrubs from Britain, Canada, Australia, India and Holland to be planted and the area is still tended lovingly by local people. It was Len who took many of the official photographs of this event. Certainly worth a visit if you are in the Tokyo region of Japan. (Quilliam, 1998)

At the same time, there were other Remembrance Services taking place in Britain, including one at Coventry Cathedral where the theme was reconciliation. Although we know this is not something that all FEPOWs are seeking, it was a very poignant example of efforts by so many people. Coventry has particular links with Japan as they both have identical statues "Reconciliation" on public display since 1995.

As well as Mrs Keiko Holmes and Mr Philip Malins speaking, there were moving addresses by three ex-FEPOWs plus a broadcast link with Mr Koshi Kobayashi in Hiroshima who spoke of a young girl who developed leukemia following the atom bomb in 1945, and a former Japanese POW interpreter Mr Nagasi who asked for forgiveness of his role at the time.

This is just an example of some of the initiatives over the years, including efforts by individual Japanese people. For instance, while Mr Mick Morley had been captured and shot in the leg, many years later in 1989 a Japanese man visiting Edinburgh asked a local Reverend if he would give a gift of £50 to "a deserving old soldier who'd been a Jap POW" as he was sorry for the treatment they received (So the Jap just wanted to say sorry, 1989).

Of course, much of the action is seen with scepticism, especially when it is linked with politicians such as Tony Blair. A very controversial article appeared in the Sun newspaper January 14th 1998 as they published a piece that was prepared by Premier Ryutaro Hashimoto to speak to the British public about reconciliation.

A critical point he made was the reference to what his predecessor had said in 1995 (that they refused to acknowledge Japan as an aggressor during WWII), going on to formally express *"our feelings of deep remorse and heartfelt apology for the tremendous damage and suffering of that time"*. He also stated how wonderful the newly-forged links with Britain were, and especially how much he admired Tony Blair – not necessarily a view shared by everyone!

They also planned to increase the number of pilgrimages on offer, noting *"This will not bring back the dead. But I hope the British people will see it in the spirit in which it is intended –*

one of reconciliation and peace and hopes for the future"
(Hashimoto, 1998).

By the beginning of 2001, a group of Japanese film-makers
led by Akinori Suzuki were planning to break their taboo
about discussing the plight of FEPOWs, determined to *"bring
home to a younger generation [of Japanese] a painful legacy
which a progressive post-war nation in a state of denial has
kept hidden"*. He had been appalled by the discovery of 200
prisoners' dog tags unearthed at Osaka Castle and so had
started his research.

Clearly, there are many British ex-POWs who were reluctant
to meet him, or indeed refused point-blank. As a veteran

POW Norman Wright said at this time, "I am a Christian. I can forgive, though I shall never forget" (Macaulay, 2001). As with any references to the need for peace, events that happened more than 70 years ago cannot be blamed on the younger generations who have little knowledge of what happened in the name of War.

For some, there is no reconciliation possible.

7. Remembrance

War Graves

Len Harrap provided a very interesting history of the Commonwealth War Cemetery I visited at Yokohama (Harrap, 1994). He explains that *"the task of burying and reporting military casualties on foreign soil in wartime falls on the unit [military unit involved]. After which the Army Graves Service locates and registers each individual grave and, if necessary, moves it to a permanent location"*.

Unlike some other countries, Commonwealth policy was not to repatriate the dead but to bury them where they fell with comrades of the same campaign. The War Graves Commission ensured that 1,100,000 men and women who died in WWI were named and subsequently, over 600,000 from WWII. Because of this policy, they now have several thousand sites around the world to look after.

The Treaty signed in 1951 required Japan to provide an appropriate burial place for victims of war who died there, and the site was agreed in 1955. By 1957, agreement had been reached through a joint committee from both sides to ensure the site was maintained and administered properly.

From my visit, I can confirm it is a peaceful environment where visitors can rest and reflect in private. The War Graves Commission will send a photograph of a grave or cemetery if a family member requests it (there is a fee but check what that is at present). It should also be noted that COFEPOW has a library with details of many cemeteries and names of those buried there, so you can also contact them for specific information.

Memorials

There are many Memorials to the prisoners who worked and died during captivity in the Far East. As noted earlier, Keiko Holmes' efforts on behalf of ex-FEPOWs resulted from seeing the memorial raised for those who had worked in the copper mine in Iruku, likely to include my father.

The JEATH museum is the open-air museum built in Kanchanaburi, Thailand in memory of those who worked on the "Death Railway" and the River Kwai bridge. It is based on the style of a typical hut POWs lived in and houses photos and artefacts from this terrible period of the war. It is interesting that their leaflet makes a point of saying it

"has been constructed not for the maintenance of the hatred among human beings, especially among the Japanese and the allied countries, but to warn and teach us the lesson of HOW TERRIBLE WAR IS. MAY PEACE ALWAYS CONQUER VIOLENCE"

The JEATH war museum

History.

JEATH museum is an open air museum. Its structure is also a realistic construction of an actual (P.O.W.s) hut. It was established in 1977 by the present chief abbot of Wat Chaichumpol., Ven. Phra Theppanyasuthee. This museum is now runs by the temple.

JEATH museum was established to collect thevarious items connected with the construction of the Death Railway by the prisoners of war (P.O.W.s) in the second world war, during 1942–1943. (2485–2486 B.E.)

(1) The first thing you will see when you arrive at the museum is the bamboo hut with the collection of photographs. It is the hut which is very similar to the prisoners' camp where the prisoners of war had lived while they were forced by the Japanese army to construct the Death Railway linking Thailand and Burma.

Actually, the hut is not an original, but it is completely built in the model of an original one. Here you will see how the prisoners lived while they were working.

(2) Secondly, we exhibit many photographs taken in the real situations by Thais and prisoners of war. The Japanese did not object to photographs in the beginning although later they prohibited prisoners from taking photographs or making any kind of records because of the bad reflection on them. There are also many articles written by ex–prisoners still alive, their relatives, their friends and writers who interviewed many prisoners, to demonstrate the suffering of the prisoners.

(3) Thirdly, there are many items such as pistols, knives, helmets, water canteens etc. which were used by P.O.W.s. Here you will also see a large bomb dropped to destroy the bridge over the River Kwae and the railway tract to stop the transportation of the Japanese army between Thailand and Burma.

We call it the JEATH museum for the abbreviation of the name of the six countries involved; Japan (J), England (E), America and Australia (A), Thailand (T), and Holland (H). The Japanese were the controllers of the railway project, Thailand was involved as the conquer country, the other 4 countries were involved as P.O.W.s, with the actual constructions of the 415 kilometers long Death Railway and the bridge over the River Kwae.

The Kwai Railway Memorial museum and library was built at Hell Fire Pass by the Australian government as an official memorial to the workers of the railway. It was noted in 1997 that the British government would not support the project financially (Stubbs, 1997), and even by the end of that year, they were still refusing to add any assistance as "it had never been Government policy in this country to contribute to Memorials".

However, this is not strictly true – they appear to have just been a bit picky about which ones they do support! For instance, Tony Blair's government did contribute to the memorial for those who perished in the Potato Famine.

The only church in the UK dedicated to prisoners held captive in the Far East is FEPOW Memorial Church of Our Lady & St Thomas of Canterbury in Wymondham, Norfolk. They hold more than 25,000 names of those who died in captivity and hold an annual memorial service.

FEPOW MEMORIAL CHURCH
of
OUR LADY AND ST. THOMAS OF CANTERBURY
The Presbytery, 1 Norwich Road, Wymondham, Norfolk, NR18 0QE
Tel. & Fax: (01953) 603104 website<http://www.fepow-memorial.org.uk>

THE DEBT
OF HONOUR
WE OWE

The refurbished FEPOW Memorial
Chapel

Message from Father David Jennings, Priest - Custodian of the FEPOW Memorial Church

Dear Friends,

When Dr. Lewis Moonie, the Parliamentary under-secretary of State for Defence announced on the Government's behalf, the ex-gratia payment of £10,000 to each surviving Far East Prisoner of War or their surviving spouse, he rightly reminded the whole nation of the 'Debt of Honour' we owe to those prisoners, because what happened to them was so appalling that it has remained with them for the rest of their lives.

The 'Debt of Honour we owe' has a special significance here at the FEPOW Memorial Church. Day by day and week by week people come to Wymondham to offer their prayer of Remembrance at the newly restored and enhanced Memorial. As I can personally testify, many come to view a name recently added to the memorial books; which was omitted in the original compilation, or of those who survived their internment and died in the years that followed. All are remembered here for the suffering they endured and for the peace they now enjoy.

Our simple little Church stands as a sign that, while generations come and go, the Remembrance of those who suffered is honoured. Father Malcom Cowin who began the work some fifty years ago and himself a survivor wrote the following. It sums up the reason for the memorial.

They died in misery, often in agony,
upon no bed
with nothing but a sack to cover them
in squalor unbelievable.

Here is the symbol of things
they never knew in their last days -
peace, quiet, cleanliness
and the cool, soft air of prayer -
a living memorial -
God's house built in their memory.

With every blessing and renewed thanks for your support.

The National Memorial Arboretum in Alrewas, England is a wonderful example of a permanent reminder that also presents a message of peace. It took many years in the planning to get the site up and running and has steadily developed since it was first planned many years ago. Each distinct area representing the different arms of the Forces plus other related organisations, is now (2015) well established. For FEPOWs, there are poignant reminders of groups of prisoners and different camps where they were held.

The first tree was planted in the Burma Star and Far East Grove in August 1998, and a section of the Burma railway track is installed there. Queen Elizabeth, the Queen Mother, opened the Field of Remembrance on 9th November 2000 and it was officially opened in May 2001.

This is a fantastic site – again, a restful beautifully landscaped garden and also a well-established Memorial building to hold evidence of the lives of prisoners and their families during the war. COFEPOW is particularly interested in maintaining this memorial and adding to its historical archive so contact them for more information. (Cooper, 1999).

8. Conclusions

Terry Waite said recently you "discover a strength within yourself you never knew you had" 24/8/14.

Other conflicts

Although the focus of this book is on prisoners of war held in the Far East, there are always some similarities to draw with later conflicts elsewhere. Whatever the treatment of the POWs, the lack of information about their location, and the uncertainty about when and if they will come home, is a common feature for the families.

When I started to ask ex-POWs and families if they would like to contribute to this book with their personal memories, I was very thankful for all the statements they could provide, brief or detailed. In 1991, I received a letter from F.Linaker who lived in Manchester – he had been captured by the Germans and taken prisoner in the Western Desert in 1942.

Although a different war arena, he too had to endure meagre rations and enforced long-distance marches across difficult terrain. For him, it was in the freezing cold winter of 1944-45 from Poland, through Czechoslovakia to Bavaria over 3 months. Many other POWs with him died, including Russian POWs who just "didn't exist" to the Germans.

As with FEPOWs, his wife did not know where he was for more than 6 months and finally saw a photograph of him with other POWs in the Manchester Evening News. He thinks his wife found it extremely traumatic – as he says, they were very young and naive and had only been married for 11 months before he left.

She had a lot of support from family, but it all became even more distressing when her brother was taken prisoner in Singapore and died while working on the Thai-Burma railway. He was just so thankful that she waited for him as this gave him hope to get through his experiences. He says how some of the other POWs had nothing to look forward to, their wives having left them *"or had got pregnant. Terrible letters some got"*.

When these POWs arrived back in the UK, there was no mention of them by the government or the press, they just received a new uniform, were fed and given travel warrants then sent home with the standard 42 days compassionate leave. In his case, he says he received excellent medical care from hospital, psychiatric staff, physiotherapists and his GP. There are many parallels with FEPOWs, although the level of medical care they received seems to have been very hit and miss depending on where they lived.

At this time, I also spoke with Suzanne Hardiman from Worcester whose husband was taken hostage in Iraq. When her husband was taken, she went to the Embassy and they said her letters would get to him, but she knows that only 3 reached him and the rest were burned.

It was better when the Red Cross got involved, but she thought the Foreign Office "was useless" as they would not believe her when she got letters from him saying they had all been moved to the Installation sites. In addition, all the wives of the hostages thought Mrs Thatcher's broadcast just made the whole situation worse. Although Suzanne felt compelled to watch the news broadcasts, they did make her feel more frightened but she had to watch in case she saw him. This is the same time that the Lockwood family (also from Worcester) were being held and the little boy was shown standing next to Saddam Hussain.

Money was not such a great problem for her as his firm continued to pay his salary and kept a job for him when he came back. She did have a huge telephone bill of £200 to pay but the local Rugby Club gave her some money too. As we have seen, this is a more positive attitude than many FEPOWs found on their return, although the government does not appear to have improved much in its support!

On his return, "he had lost a lot of weight, looked gaunt, and had that lost look in his eyes". It is interesting to see how they coped on his return – she wanted him to stay in to have more time together, but he wanted to go out and "get back to normal". It had also been her life that had changed, and there was now the issue of both being more independent – who put the lights off, locked up each night.

1991 was a busy year for the release of hostages who had been held captive for several years. Another hostage of Saddam Hussain, Clive Stringer, committed suicide after being held for four months. His wife said "the real Clive never came home" (SUN 24/7/91).

Saddam hostage suicide

TRAGIC Clive Stringer blasted himself to death with a shotgun after becoming depressed over being held as an Iraqi "human shield," an inquest heard yesterday. Mr Stringer, 47, suffered mood swings after four months as Saddam Hussein's captive. Widow Pauline, 45, of St Ives, Cornwall, said: "The real Clive never came home." Verdict: Suicide.

THE SUN, Wednesday, July 24, 1991   15

Wife keeps hopes alive for 'forgotten' Beirut captive

Jackie Mann was released after being captured in Beirut, although given his "true-grit Brit" reputation, most people who knew him thought his captors might have got a worse deal than they had expected! But his wife had had no news of where he was, why he was captured or, indeed, whether he was still alive.

John McCarthy and Terry Waite had also been held captive for around 5 years, and publicity revolved around regular pressure from families and friends of the hostages given the perceived lack of effort by our own government. However Douglas Hurd did make a point of publicly demanding (The Independent 1991) the freeing of hostages in the Middle East stating this was *"because I know some people feel the Foreign*

Office is so concerned with other things that it forgets those [5] people".

Hurd demands freeing of hostages

DOUGLAS HURD sought yesterday to dispel suggestions of Foreign Office lethargy over the British hostages in the Middle East with a public demand for their early release, *writes John Pienaar*.

The Foreign Secretary warned that Iran's failure to procure the release of Terry Waite, John McCarthy and Jack Mann was an obstacle to improved relations between Britain and Iran. He also told the conference that Britain was pressing hard for the release of Ian Richter, the businessman charged with spying in Iraq, and Douglas Brand, an engineer.

Later, the Foreign Secretary said he had expressed his concern for the hostages "up-front, because I know some people feel the Foreign Office is so concerned with other things that it forgets those five people".

Mr Hurd's speech emphasised the Government's wish to see a UN "police force" in Iraq to protect Kurdish refugees, and reiterated Britain's willingness to hold military exercises, and occasionally deploy RAF aircraft, to help underpin regional security.

On the European Community, Mr Hurd sought to assuage Tory fears that the Government's co-operative approach to the EC meant no surrender of British interests. "We want to ensure that the Community is only involved in policies where objectives cannot be achieved by individual states acting at national level," he said.

The Western European Union was capable of acting as a bridge between EC heads of government and Nato. But the UK would not accept majority voting within the Community as the basis for forming a common foreign policy. "That would have led to paralysis over the Gulf," he said.

American hostage Edward Tracy was released after 5 years in captivity in Syria, but made light of this long term by praising the cooking talents of his captors, much to the surprise of the Press (The Independent 12/8/91). However, this release of Tracy meant that another hostage held for the same length of time, Mr Cicippio, a financial adviser, was not so lucky. His wife had waited in the shadows to see which of the two men was to be released. Sadly, she still had no news of him as it was Mr Tracy they brought out. Her wait continued.

Tracy makes light of his captivity

At the same time, in 1991 the Gulf War had ended and as the soldiers returned home, the incidence of violent outbursts related to PTSD increased dramatically. Press coverage shows too many examples of violence towards a partner or parent (Todd, 1991). How does this differ from FEPOWs? Clearly, as a prisoner, they had already had their fighting spirit broken to some extent, so it was more about finding ways to deal with the tormented memories of harm to themselves rather than their harm to the other side in combat.

Government failings post-war

The general feeling has always been that everyone in the Far East area of conflict was let down by incompetence and lack of any "expertise", including the *"low standard of some of the troop reinforcements which arrived late in the day" (Elphick, 1995)*. The loss of Singapore in particular was seen as *"a critical event in world politics shattering the myth of white superiority and the end of European empire-building in the East"*.

Strong sentiments stated by Elphick, but he is not the only one to express such thoughts. For example, the exhibition flyer for Jack Chalker's images (Chalker) also refers to the *"constant irritant to many ex-FEPOWs that British Governments post war consistently, and perhaps deliberately, avoided any open enquiry or Royal Commission to investigate the gross military and civil complacency, and negligence, on the part of British Command in Malaya which led to its fall and that of Singapore"*.

It goes on to suggest that this *"led to the greatest and most ignominious defeat in British history and a period of unrelieved horror for the Chinese and Malay civilian population for the following four years"*. This wider impact on the local civilian population is often overlooked as they, too, were brutally treated by the Japanese.

The critical question of why no inquiry into what is described as such a disaster does not actually seem to have been answered even now in 2015.

Elphick presents some strong arguments behind this lack of action by the government of the time and in the following years. He cites that on 23rd April 1942 the Prime Minister, Churchill, said it would not be good for the country if there was a Royal Commission Inquiry, citing the need to focus on the continuing war efforts rather than the inevitable recriminations. He did suggest there might be some inquiry if/when the war was won. The USA planned its own inquiry into Pearl Harbour in 1945. (Elphick, 1995)

There are some inconsistences in Churchill's stance as he did insist on an inquiry into the fall of Crete in 1941 – although it also appears to some commentators that its findings were suppressed. Even while he was still in power 1951-1955 there was no inquiry.

According to records, and the book by historian Raymond Callahan, "Churchill's personal policy consisted of relying on America and hoping for the best!" Clearly this is opinion and interpretation by that author, but who knows! Elphick also makes an interesting reference to a meeting of British and Australian historians in 1953 to reach a consensus on what actually took place. There appear to be many documents quoted by him that refer obliquely to the acceptance of some "watering down and other modifications" to the publication of facts. He gives the example – not to "throw aspersions on the leaders". We can see why there was such dismay by ex-FEPOWs who felt everything was being swept under the carpet – but remember the scathing attack on actions by the American administration too (Critchley, 1991)

The Japanese carried out a lot of intelligence gathering in Singapore and Malaya, but the British had a "non-provocation policy" so did little to deal with any potential threat. As we have seen from several sources, there was a lack of awareness or recognition of Japanese military capabilities; a lack of coordination in strategy, thinking and communication; and the two top British Generals in the region held diametrically-opposing views.

There were even disagreements within the War Committee on defence policy, specifically the lack of defences on the northern coast of Singapore island. They even disagreed about how to word a telegram to Churchill voicing their concerns, in the end sending a much-watered down version.

So, in 1940 Churchill made the decision not to focus on Malaya as he was convinced that Singapore was a "fortress" and that the Japanese threat was not severe. He believed they were unlikely to send the necessary large military force that would be needed to attack.

Alongside this lack of awareness, and the Americans' refusal to take notice of the intelligence warnings about a plan to strike Pearl Harbour, the British and Australian forces relied heavily on the US presence in the region. As we know, within two weeks of the Australian forces arriving in Singapore, they were taken prisoner.

After such a devastating conflict, there will always be criticism voiced about what the government did or did not do at the time. According to many FEPOWs, successive British governments consistently refused to instigate any public inquiries or Royal Commission on the gross military and civil negligence which led to the fall of Malaya and Singapore. It has been quoted (Chalker) that "critical facts have been blandly smothered in a mass of technical detail in official British war histories", particularly during early post-war years. Such government insensitivity is best demonstrated by the bill sent to a former FEPOW for non-return of uniform (greatcoat)!

Supporting each other

There are few FEPOWs left alive, but the associations keep going to give them the support they need. Although the Royal British Legion has been there for ex-service personnel for many years, FEPOWs were initially banned from forming their own groups and speaking publicly about their experiences. However, given the lack of specialist support and recognition of what they had been through, former FEPOWs soon found it helpful to meet and talk with others who knew.

Very soon, formal constitutions were established and regional groups formed the backbone of FEPOW support as well as groups such as Japanese Labour Camp Survivors Association (JLCSA) and their Fulcrum newsletter. As everyone gets older, of course, the children of FEPOWs have become more involved and COFEPOW was formed to help existing group members and ensure their needs are met. After all, the remaining POWs are now in late 80s, 90s and even over 100 years old.

Several people have recorded their personal stories and published memoirs (see list of publications), often referring to the pain suffered by family back home who knew nothing about what was happening. As most of the children of FEPOWs reach retirement age, this additional source of evidence will start to dwindle too.

This book is intended to be a testament to everyone that was affected by the long, savage imprisonment of our military personnel fighting for what we have today, many of them like my father just teenagers. They were not just British, of course, as many American and Canadian, Australian, Dutch and New Zealanders were imprisoned in the Far East region.

It is important that the wider impact on families and friends is also recognised as they too were suffering.

"Many is the time at the bedside of a dying man he has asked me to pray for his death, for his peace, for release from his abject misery."
Painting by POW Eric Stacy

What of the Death Railway? While the main construction was completed in 1943, some POWs and local workers were needed to keep the supplies moving along the track. In 1945, Allied bombers destroyed several sections of the track around Brenkasi yard. While people had run for cover, the Japanese decided to move up the line to the Three Pagoda Pass.

POWs apparently went back to their camp, now guarded by the Koreans rather than the Japanese who had gone to Kanchanaburi. Basically, what was left of the track was ripped up by the local Thai people, bits being sold on to the Thai rail authorities – a nice touch!

In the 1980s, an Australian company started work there, found the train engine hidden inside a cave and transported it to the Museum at Kanchanaburi. This is also where skeleton remains of prisoners of war are held. (Lane, 2001)

There are still many more examples of what happened in different camps and the heroic actions of prisoners who had to **"live for the day and control imagination"** (Terry Waite).

To you all – we salute you!

9. Further information

Support Groups and contacts – there are so many around to choose from – the easiest way is to search online.

- NFFWRA – National FEPOW Fellowship Welfare Remembrance Association
- Local FEPOW associations such as Birmingham Association of FEPOW
- COFEPOW – Children of Far East Prisoners of War http://www.cofepow.org.uk/ - you can get more details on-line (currently with an interim chairman so contact details may change)
- BURMA STAR ASSOCIATION www.burmastar.org.uk/ -they may be updating their site but still publish a newsletter. Email burmastar@btconnect.com. PE Crawley MBE, Administrator/Editor DEKHO!, Burma Star Association, 34 Grosvenor Gardens, London SW1W 0DH, Tel: 0207 8234273
- RBL -The Royal British Legion's Head Office and postal address is 199 Borough High Street London SE1 1AA http://www.britishlegion.org.uk/about-us/
- The Java FEPOW Club – Margaret Martin Secretary & Welfare officer - margaretmartin2@sky.com
- https://fepowhistory.wordpress.com/ -

- http://www.iwm.org.uk/
- http://nationalfepowfellowship.org.uk/

- http://www.thenma.org.uk/
- www.far-eastern-heroes.org.uk
- www.fepow-community.org.uk/
- www.fepow-news.com
-

- **British Red Cross UK Office address**

British Red Cross

UK Office

44 Moorfields

London EC2Y 9AL

Tel: 0844 871 11 11 (+ 44 2071 3879 00 from abroad)

Fax: 020 7562 2000

Textphone: 020 7562 2050

http://www.redcross.org.uk/About-us

Official Records of personnel, places of captivity, burial sites

- There are research groups around the UK and further afield, such as Researching FEPOW History Group
- The next page gives some specific details about ships sunk while carrying POWs – the Birmingham FEPOW Association is particularly knowledgeable on this data.

SHIPS SUNK WHILST CARRYING PRISONERS

MONTEVIEDO MARU - 1053 POWs on board (presume American). Sunk 1.7.42 by submarine east of Luzon, Phillipines. No survivors. (Ref JLCSA Fulcrum)

LISBON MARU - 1816 UK and Canadian POWs on board being transported from Hong Kong to Japan. Sunk 2.10.42. by US Submarine Growler. Survivors 977. Died 839 (Ref PRO CO980/224).

NICHIMEI MARU - 1000 Dutch POWs on board being transported from Java via Singapore to Moulmein, Burma. Sunk 15.1.43 by aircraft. Survivors 961. Died 39 (Ref PRO CO980/224).

SUEZ MARU - 548 UK and Dutch POWs on board being transported from Ambon (Mulukan Islands) to Java. Sunk 29.11.43 by US Submarine Bonefish near island of Kangean, north of Bali. No survivors. (Ref PRO CO980 224) (US Submarine Bonefish later lost)

TAMAHOKO MARU - 772 Australian, Dutch, UK and US POWs on board being transported from Java to Japan. Sunk 24.6.44 by US Submarine Tang in Nagasaki Bay. Survivors 212. Died 560. (Ref PRO CO980/224) (US Submarine Tang later lost)

HARAGIKU/HARIKIKU MARU (otherwise known as VAN WAERWIJCK) - 720 UK and Dutch POWs on board being transported from Medan, Sumatra, to Pakanbaru, Sumatra. Sunk 26.6.44 by HM Submarine Truculent near Belawan, Sumatra. Survivors 543. Died 177 (Ref PRO CO980/224).

OSAKA/ASAKA MARU - 750 UK and Australian POWs on board being transported from Thailand via Singapore to Japan. Sunk 13.8.44 by Typhoon off Formosa. Survivors 700. Died 50 (Ref London FEPOW Post).

SHINYO MARU - 750 POWs on board (presume American). Sunk 17.9.44 by submarine off Mindanao, Philippines (Ref JLCSA Fulcrum).

ZUNYO/JUNYO MARU - 2200 Dutch and UK POWs on board being transported from Java to Pedang, Sumatra. Sunk 18.8.44 by HM Submarine Tradewind near Moeko Moeko, Sumatra. Survivors 723. Died 1477. (Ref PRO CO980/224)

RAKUYO MARU - 1318 UK and Australian POWs on board being transported from Thailand via Singapore to Japan. Sunk 12.9.44 by US Submarine Sealion. Japanese vessel Kibibi Maru picked up 136. US submarines picked up 159 from both the Kachidoki Maru and the Rakuyo Maru (of who 7 died). Deaths from both ships (excluding those on US submarines) 1403 (Ref John and Clay Blair "Return from the River Kwai") (US Submarine Sealion later lost)

and KACHIDOKI MARU - 900 UK and Australian POWs on board being transported from Thailand via Singapore to Japan. Sunk 12.9.44 by US Submarine Pampanito. Japanese vessel Kibibi Maru picked up 520. US submarines picked up 159 from both the Kachidoki Maru and the Rakuyo Maru (of who 7 died). Deaths from both ships (excluding those on US submarines) 1403. (Ref as for Rakuyo Maru)

UNNAMED SHIP - 150 UK and Dutch POWs on board being transported from Ambon, Mulukan Islands, to Java. Sunk 20.9.44 by aircraft off Muna Island, S of Celebes. Survivors 138 picked up by Maros Maru also transporting POWs from Ambon to Java.). (Ref PRO AIR2/6955/5299) (NB Fl Lt Denis Mason was awarded the George Medal for his actions during the sinking of this ship)

TOYOFUKU MARU - 1287 UK, Australian and Dutch POWs on board being transported from Thailand via Singapore to Japan. After breaking down and remaining in Manila, Phillipines, for two months sunk on 21.9.44 by aircraft 5 miles off Manilla. Survivors 380. Died 907 (Ref London FEPOW Post and JLCSA Fulcrum)

ARISAN MARU - 1782 POWs (presume American) on board being transported from Phillipines to Japan. Sunk 24.10.44 Bashi Straits, near Taiwan. No survivors. (Ref JLCSA Fulcrum)

JAPANESE TRANSPORT NO 125 - 104 UK and Dutch POWs from the Mulukan Islands on board being transported from Muna Island, S of Celebes, to Java. Sunk by aircraft about 7 miles off Muna. Survivors 77. Dead 27. (Ref PRO Air2/6955/5299)

ORYOKU MARU - Sunk 15.12.44 off Battan Philippines (ref P Dunstan)

ENQOURA MARU - Sunk 26.3.45 by land based aircraft 50 miles SW Formosa. (ref P Dunstan)

BRAZIL MARU - Sunk 12.5.45 by mine Inland Sea of Japan. (ref P Dunstan)

Bibliography – references used in preparing this book

Archbold, H. (1989, February 26th). Ex-British POWs fight for torture cash. *The Sunday Telegraph*.

Archbold, H. (1989, February 26th). Ex-British POWs fight for torture cash. *The Sunday Telegraph*.

Archer, B. &. (2015). Quilt Studies. *Journal of the British Quilt Study Group*, Issue 16.

Arnold, H. (1989, February 24th). Japs jibe at Queen. *The Sun*, p. 2 (front page & page 2).

Arnold, H. (1989, February 25th). We are nod amused. *The Sun*, p. 2.

Brooks, R. (1999). The March from Katong House to Changi Jail. *COFEPOW Newsletter 4th Edition*, pp. pages 13-14.

Bulloch, J. (1991, September 25th). True-grit Brit a test for kidnappers' will. *The Independent*, p. 1.

Butterworth, J. -E. (1991, May/June). the Man Behind the Bridge. *Oldham & District FEPOW Association newsletter 89*, pp. pages 2-3.

Chalker, J. Images as a Japanese Prisoner of War. *February 1998*. The Daiwa Anglo-Japanese Foundation, London.

Clements, P. (2001). Sticky Dewi. Blackie & Co Publishers

Cooper, C. (1999). *Memorial to the Far east Prisoner of War.*

Cooper, C. -E. (1999, April). History in the Making. *COFEPOW Newsletter 4th Edition*, pp. pages 5-7.

Cooper, C. -e. (1999, April). The story of the Changi Quilts. *COFEPOW Newsletter 4th edition*, p. page 12.

Cordingly, E. (2015). *Down to Bedrock.* Art angels Publishing Ltd.

Cordingly, L. (2015). *The Changi Cross.* Art Angels Publishing Ltd.

Cornwell, R. (1991, November 9th). Congress to delve into hostage row. *the Independent*, p. 1.

Critchley, J. (1991, November 16th). Julian Critchley on the Lessons of Pearl Harbour. *The Independent Magazine*, p. 1.

Davison, P. (1991, August 12th). Tracy makes light of his captivity. *The Independent*, p. 1.

Davison, P. a. (1991, August 12th). McCarthy fulfils his mission. *The Independent*, p. 1 (front page).

Dhillon, S. (1989, January 18th). Forgive - even if you can't forget. *dorset Evening Echo*, p. 1 (Letters to the Editor).

Duckworth, J. N. (1999, April). Japanese Holiday. *COFEPOW Newsletter 4th edition*, pp. Pages 9-10.

Editor. (1988). All-party support for Bruce's POW fight. *Dorset Evening Echo*, p. 1.

Editor. (1988, May 12th). What price suffering? *Dorset Evening Echo*, p. 1 (Comment).

Editor. (1989, March 20th). Army in Jap jeeps shock. *Daily Star*, pp. 3 (front cover, page 2, page 8 comment).

Editor. (1989, February 25th). Editorial: Lest we Forget - Emperor Horohito 1901-1989. *The Sun*.

Editor. (2002, January). The Cost of Captivity. *COFEPOW Newsletter 15th Edition*, p. page 6.

editor, C. (2002, January). The Happiness Box. *Chidren and Families of the Far East Prisoners of War Newsletter 15th edition*, p. page 12.

Elphick, P. (1995). *Singapore: The Impregnable Fortress.* Hodder & Stoughton.

Foley, J. (2014, August 24th). interview with Terry Waite. *Mail on Sunday*.

Freeman, F. (n.d.). *Memories as FEPOW in Java and Sumatra.*

Hall, A. (1991, July 19th). Are these men still prisoners 20 years after Vietnam war? *The Sun*, p. page 9.

Harrap, L. (1994, December). The Commonwealth Remembers its War dead. *Sundays (published Japan)*, p. page 3.

Harris, p. (1997, May 24th). The New Offensive. *Daily Mail*, p. front page.

Harris, P. (1997, May 24th). The new offensive - Cook presses Japan on cash for PoWs. *Daily Mail*, p. front page.

Harrop, L. (1994, December). The Commonwealth Remembers its War Dead. *? Foreign Community Newsletter*, p. page 3.

Hashimoto, R. (1998, January 14th). Britain and Japan must go forward together. *The Sun*, p. page 6.

Holtham, C. -e. (1988, July/August). Prisoner of War (Compensation) Motion proposed. *FEPOW Fulcrum Newsletter 24*, pp. Pages 1-3.

Holtham, C. -E. (1989, June/July). Pilgrimage to the Far East. *FEPOW Fulcrum*, p. page 4.

Hughes, S. (1991, April 11th). spare a thought today for the hell of John McCarthy. *The Sun*, pp. 18, 23.

Iraqi hostage clung to his [OU] units from Kuwait to Mosul. (1991, May). *Sesame (OU)*, pp. 6-7.

Japan Information & Cultural Centre (Embassy of Japan). (1997, November 25th). Initiatives for Reconciliation and Friendship. *JAPAN No 643*, p. Front page.

Jennings, D. -c. (2000). The debt of Honour we owe. *FEPOW Memorial Church newsletter*, p. 4 page booklet.

Jeynes, J. (1991, April 5th). Writer turns spotlight on plight of captives. *Worcester Evening News*, p. page 10.

Lane, A. (2001, May/June). Work on the Death Railway. *NESA News*, p. page 5.

Lucas, E. (1991, May 4th). Bush denies involvement in hostage scandal. *Independent*.

Macaulay, D. (2001, February 22nd). Japan tuning in to atrocity. *Eastern Daily Press*, p. centre page spread.

Marlin, J. (2015). My 3.5 years in internment, Singapore 15/2/42 to 15/8/45.

Maslin, S. (1989 , March 4th). The cruellest insult of all. *Dorset Evening Echo*, p. Letters to the Editor.

Mason, P. (1991, August 13th). Gulf Diary of a heroic bomber pilot. *The Sun*, p. 4 page supplement.

Matthews, T. (1993). *Shadows Dancing, Japanese Espionage against the West 1939-45*. Robert Hale.

McKee, V. (1991, January). FREE! When a hostage comes home. *Good Housekeeping*, pp. 56-59.

Morris, J. (1987). But to the Grave: Hostages of Fortune. *Saturday Night*, 23-32.

Naylor, M. (2012). *Talk to Catenian Association "Liberation from captivity by Japanese WWII"*.

Numata, S. (1997). *Britain & Japan: A Diplomat's Eye.* Anglo-Japanese Economic Institute.

Office, T. W. (September 1945). *To All British Army Ex-Prisoners of War.*

Old comrades in protest. (1989, February). *Dorset Evening Echo*, p. editorial.

O'Sullivan, J. (n.d.). Bush visit to Hirohito funeral signals orgy of Japan-bashing. *Independent?*

Partridge, J. (2001, May/June). Massacre at Alexandra. *NESA News*, p. page 9.

Pienaar, J. (1991). Hurd demands freeing of hostages. *The Independent*.

Quilliam, T. (1998, April). Jacqueline Jeynes' visit to Yokohama War Cemetery. *Birmingham Association of FEPOW Newsletter 59*, p. page 4.

Ryan, B. (1988, May 11th). Dorset POWs join in compensation battle. *Dorset Evening Echo*, p. 1.

Ryan, B. (1988, May 16th). MP backs POW's cash campaign. *Dorset Evening Echo*, p. 1.

Ryan, B. (1989, May 11th). Dorset POWs join in compensation battle. *Dorset Evening Echo*, p. 1.

Saddam hostage suicide. (1991, July 24th). *The Sun*, p. page 15.

Sayid, R. (1991, April 18th). Tribute to John. *The Sun*.

Seiker, F. (1995). *Lest We Forget.* Worcester UK: Bevere Vivis Gallery Books Ltd.

Skee, G. W. (n.d.). *Song That Bridged the Gap: A Yuletide War Memory.* Copy at Royal Scots Museum, Edinburgh Castle.

So the Jap just wanted to say sorry. (1989, December 31st). *The Sunday Post*, p. page 20.

Stubbs, I. (1997, March). Fred Seiker author of Lest We Forget. *Brimingham Association of FEPOW Newsletter 55*, p. page 4.

Stubbs, L. (1997, January). Kwai Railway Memorial. *Birmingham Association of FEPOW newsletter 54*, p. page 2.

Stubbs, L. (1998, January). Mrs Keiko Holmes. *Brimingham Association of FEPOW newsletter 58*, pp. page 6-7.

Stubbs, L. -e. (1997, July). Letter to Editor Daily Telegraph: Japanese Money. *Birmingham Association of FEPOW*, pp. pages 3-4.

Tett, D. (2002). *A Postal History of the Prisoners of War & Civilian Internees in East Asia during the Second World War.* Stuart Rossiter Trust Fund/ BFA Publishing.

Titherington, A. -e. (1997, Spring). Bits & Pieces: Hidden Horrors - Japanese War Crimes in World War II. *Fulcrum - Japanese Labour Camp Survivors Association Issue 51*, p. page 6.

Todd, R. a. (1991, July 30th). Wives who lose their men after war is won. *Daily Mirror.*

Tsuji, M. (1997). *The Capture of Singapore: Japan's Greatest Victory, Britain's Worst Defeat.* Spellman Ltd.

Walker, J. a. (1960, July 10). Glasgow Postie's Amazing Experience on a Doomed Ship. *The Sunday Post*, p. page 11.

Ward, J. (1999, April). Ottowa gives Hong Kong veterans $18 million. *COFEPOW Newsletter 4th Edition*, p. page 11.

Ward, S. (1991, April 13th). Wife keeps hopes alive for 'forgotten' Beirut captive. *The Independent*, p. page 8.

Warner, L. &. (1982). *Women beyond the Wire: a story of prisoners of the Japanese 1942-45.* Michael Joseph Ltd.

Whymant, R. (1989, March). Rite will make Akihito sacred. *The sun.*

Wilkinson, R. (1997). *A Guest of the Japanese Government.*

Wilkinson, R. (n.d.). *A Guest of the Japanese Government.*

Wyllie, a. (1989). Duke's Hirohito funeral trip 'a slap in face'. *Dorset Evening Echo (?)*, p. ?

Wyllie, A. (1989, January 21st). Veterans to stage Hirohito protest. *Dorset Evening Echo*, p. front page.

Additional publications, though not necessarily all in print now.

2194 Days of War. (n.d.). ISBN 071120005 X.

Alexander, S. (1997 Reprint). *Sweet Kwai Run Softly.* ISBN 0 9526763 0 3.

Audus, L. (1996). *Spice Island Slaves.*

Bentinck, M. (1997). *A will to Live.*

Cosford, J. (1988: 6th Reprint 1997). *Line of Lost Lives.* ISBN 09513666 02.

Davis, P. (1991). *The Man Behind the Bridge: Brigadier Sir Phillip Toosey.* The Athlone Press.

Edwards, J. (1991). *Banzai You Bastards!* Souvenir Press Ltd.

Kelly, T. (1997). *Living With Japanese.* ISBN 09530193 0 6.

Mad Mike - A Biography of Brigadier Michael Calvert DSO. (1998). ISBN 0850525438.

Mitchell, R. K. (1997). *Forty-two months Indurance Vile.* Robert Hale Ltd.

Roberts, D. E. (1996). *No Bamboo for Coffins.*

Saddington, S. (1998). *Escape Impossible.*

Second World War. (n.d.). ISBN 000637253 8.

Stubbs, P. (2015). *Unsung Heroes of the British Army - the Far East Prisoners of WAr held in Java.*

Wall, D. (1996). *Kill the Prisoners.*

The book by David Tett referred to here is Volume 1 so others are available. He includes a very comprehensive list of other publications, many of them being personal stories from ex-FEPOWs.

About the author

Dr Jacqueline Jeynes PhD MBA B.Ed(Hons) BA(Hons)

Jacqueline is an author of non-fiction books on business and practical subjects, training programmes, and Distance Learning courses for Aberystwyth University Lifelong Learning department.

She is also a travel writer working with Silver Travel Advisor providing information on travel aimed at the 50+ age group. In 2015 she was given national recognition through the award of Writer of the Year. A series of books on walking in Wales will be published 2015-2016.

She has been married to Leslie for over 30 years, has 5 sons from her first marriage alongside Leslie's 2 daughters and a son. Incredibly, they have "approximately" 24 grandchildren plus 3 young great-grandchildren!

Dad with his great-granddaughter Lisa & great- grandson Jason in 1990